INTERNAL MIGRATION AND POPULATION REDISTRIBUTION IN INDIA

INTERNAL MIGRATION AND POPULATION REDISTRIBUTION IN INDIA

Some Reflections

N. R. PRABHAKARA

CONCEPT PUBLISHING COMPANY, NEW DELHI

First Published 1986

N.R. Prabhakara (*b* 1951-   )

Published by

Naurang Rai
Concept Publishing Company
H-13, Bali Nagar
NEW DELHI-110015 (India)

Printed in India by

Bharat Enterprises
at Chetna Printers, Shastri Marg-3
Mauzpur, Shahdara, Delhi-110053

Dedicated to
my mother
N. Nagarathnamma

PREFACE

THIS multidisciplinary comparative study of internal migration in several regions of the world is the combination of several years' collaboration by leading anthropologists, demographers, economists, and sociologists. It fills a gap in the migration literature by providing the opportunity for scholars in these fields to ask new questions and give new answers to the key problems in the study of internal migration, in a comparative context, and to address the problems in regions of varying levels of economic development, and with different economic systems.

The problem of migration is a prime example of a subject that requires the skills and approaches of scholars from several disciplines; neither the questions that must be asked nor the methods of analysis required to answer them are within the province of any single discipline. Migration statistics are used primarily to study demographic trends and their economic and social relationship.

Emigration of people from the rural areas to the cities has been a major factor of socio-economic change in developing societies. If on the one hand, emigration has acted as a feeder to urban growth, it has, on the other, played an important role in the modernization and development of the rural areas. From both the points of view the study of emigration assumes a special significance for the sociologists. Although this work is only an attempt to investigate the social and economic consequences of migration in Karnataka state (India), the findings of this work can be generalized, safely, for the rest of the country side as well.

The present study examines the relationship between population change and migration with emphasis on the changes that occur in the population redistribution. It has been generally accepted that the cause-effect relationship between population change and migration can go in either direction. That is, population change once generated has significant influence on the migration and vice-versa. That they are mutually inter-dependent and inter-acting hardly needs to be emphasized. There is need to understand the nature of these changes, and there is even greater need to unreveal the casual interrelations, if any.

Migration is a basic social process. As Durkheim has shown, in the early stages of social growth, it has been the foremost factor in the division of labour and specialisation of functions. In fact, but for migration, societies would have hardly attained the complex form of organisation they have attained today.

The author is much indebted to Dr N. Baskara Rao, Professor and Head of Population Research Centre, Institute for Social and Economic Change, for his constant help. I must also express my sincere gratitude to Dr P. Hanumantha Rayappa, Professor, Population Research Centre, I.S.E.C., for his constant encouragement.

I wish to thank Concept Publishing Company, for bringing out this book. My thanks are due to Mrs K.V. Padmalatha for her help in completing this work. I extend my thanks to Mr N. Boopathi for his excellent typing work.

N. R. PRABHAKARA

Bangalore
29 April 1985.

CONTENTS

LIST OF TABLES

1

STATEMENT OF THE PROBLEM

THE PRESENT study addresses itself to the question of the relationship between population change and migration with emphasis on the changes that occur in the economic development. Migration is as old as man himself. It is one of the principal causes, along with natural increase or decrease of population, for fluctuations in population. Migration may be motivated by various causes among which are personal, political, economic and natural forces. Migration currents acquire significant prominence with technological advance and industrial development since redistribution of population is likely to occur with development. Since migration results in the redistribution of population, its study assumes great importance in the analysis of demographic data. The object of this study is to evaluate the place of birth criterion used by census, discuss the nature and consequences of internal movements of population, rather than migration at one point of time, and consider urban areas development as a measure to control migration.

It has been generally accepted that the cause-effect relationship between population change and migration can go in either direction. That is, population change once generated has significant influence on the migration and vice-versa. That they are mutually inter-dependent and inter-acting hardly needs to be emphasized. There is need to understand the nature of these changes, and there is even greater need to unreveal the casual interrelations, if any.

Consider an area with initially high mortality and fertility, where there has been a substantial decline in mortality.[1] Assume that this decline in mortality has been due to some non-economic factors.[2] With unchanging fertility (and migration), this results in an increase in the rate of natural increase and the rate of growth of population. This increase in population may have far reaching implications on the consumption side, and after a lag of 15-20 years, when these enlarged cohorts begin to enter the productivity ages, on employment aspects as well. These new entrants to the labour force might also generate additional consumption requirements, because they would be simultaneously entering their family forming age. This might necessitate changes in various aspects of agricultural development, and migration. They could be subsumed under the following headings: (i) changes in the extent and pattern of land utilization, (ii) changes in inputs that might influence land and labour productivity, (iii) adoption and innovation of new agricultural technology, and (iv) changes in agricultural organizations such as size of holdings, land tenure, etc. To the extent that these changes bring about changes in total and per capita output, mortality, migration and fertility might be expected to change.[3]

Instead, if the initial development took place on the agricultural side, it might alter the course of mortality, fertility and migration, and as a result, rate of growth of population would be affected.[4] However, there is a growing controversy regarding the magnitude and direction of the influence of one upon the other, and this is more so with regard to the influence of population change on migration.

OBJECTIVES OF THE STUDY

The objectives of this study are two fold: first, it aims to describe and compare the patterns of population change and magnitude of migration of an area and second, it tries to clarify the nature of casual inter-relation between the change in population and migrational factors.

The recorded experience of most of today's developed countries provide the necessary data for the analysis of the inter-relation between population change and migration, during the periods of their economic and demographic transition. Moreover, the developing countries are undergoing rapid declines in mortality, with little or no change in their level of fertility. There is also said to be occurring significant changes in agriculture. The ongoing experience of these countries also provide valuable information regarding the nature of these changes, and their inter-relations under different economic, demographic, social and cultural environment.

ADVANTAGES AND LIMITATIONS OF THE STUDY

The main contributions of the study are: (i) it has tried to develop a framework within which one can analyse and compare the patterns of population change, and their components, and (ii) it has tried to provide some tentative answers to the questions of casual inter-relations between population change on the one hand and migration on the other in the context of the experience of Karnataka state and its districts during the period 1951-71. This is in addition to the information that is provided on the pattern of population change and their components.

The present study, however, has some disadvantages. Non-availability and unreliability of data have forced me to make "surmises" rather than "generalizations". At times I had to resort to very crude methods to estimate certain parameters. Even if adequate and reliable data were at hand it is difficult to make solid generalizations on the complex relationship between population change and migration and how much more difficult it would be if the data are inadequate and unreliable. If data on migration streams, and the changes therein were available then it would have been difficult to unreveal the forces behind these changes.

Given the above limitations, I would be happy if I were able to (i) present a satisfactory framework for the analysis of population and migration, (ii) present some hypothesis regarding the casual inter-relations between population change and migration, and (iii) give some rather crude indications of differences among districts with regard to population change, migration and their components.

NATURE AND TYPES OF MOVEMENT

It is necessary to consider the nature of movements of individuals rather than migration at one point of time. Often all types of movements are included under migration without any distinction, and this is misleading. First, there are seasonal movements of landless labourers and small peasants moving out of their villages to other villages and towns during the agricultural off-season looking for alternative jobs. They come back to their villages during the agricultural season. While some of them move out to find work wherever it exists, others move to the same place season after season to work with the same employer. This type of movement, although individual in character, is in the nature of trans-humance. Trans-humance occurs as an organised effort in the case of certain trading castes. For instance, in Bhotias living on the border of Nepal have two sets of villages—one on the hill tops in which they live in summer and another on the plains for winter. This cycle of movement also facilitates their trade.

Secondly, there are itinerant traders and craftsmen such as the Banjaras, the Gaddi Lohars and the Kallu Waddars who move from place to place on more or less set routes, selling country cosmetics, household and agricultural implements, and cutting stone and making grinding stones respectively. Itinerant movement is different from either trans-humance or seasonal movements; it involves several movements on longer routes and blurs the specificity of their places of origin.

Thirdly, there is a category of 'involuntary' movements which includes several variations. In marriage migration married women move from their natal villages or towns to their husband's villages and towns. In some cases (e.g., matrilineal Khasis) husbands move to wife's villages or towns. Child migration is also involuntary as children move with their parents. Government servants and others move from one place to another on transfer. Still another variation of involuntary migration occurs under extraordinary circumstances such as partition of nations, riots and floods. This may be called crisis migration. There is also displacement of persons due to a deliberate policy of the government to acquire villages for industrial purposes. Location of huge industrial plants has meant total uprooting of villages, causing out migration.

Fourthly, there is another kind of movement where people are recruited to work in plantations or in factories or in construction work through middlemen. Although indentured labour has stopped now, other forms of recruitment through agents do exist. Construction workers, for instance, move wherever the contractor moves.

Fifthly, there is the movement of commuters who are residents of villages on the fringe of cities and occasionally they may stay in their places of work for a few days. Commuting may be considered disguised migration because in the absence of their nearby village homes, they would have presumably migrated to their place of work.

Movement is neither uni-directional nor permanent. There is always movement back and forth, i.e., an adult does not move from village to the city always in steps (village-town-city), neither does he stay in the city for the rest of his life. Presence of relatives, vagaries of unemployment and retirement are some of the forces which encourage further shifts, returns and oscillations.

However, the major type of movement of people has been from rural areas to urban and especially metropolitan centres in search of employment which involves different phases and processes. Migration is brought about by a number of interacting factors and it is unwise to build mono-casual explanations in terms of distances, or the availability of opportunities at the place of destination, or the conditions of distress at the place of origin. Whether a city is near or distant, in itself is not important. Often people migrate to distant cities because they have a relative or a friend who is willing to help. Thus, a city which is physically distant, is socially near, and vice-versa. Similarly it is not always true that only the poor would migrate. It is necessary to study the decision making process in the contexts of family organisation, the stage of development of the family, dispersed kinship and friendship networks, sources and flows of information, the image of the prospective migrants about different cities, physical distances, economic situations, availability of alternative opportunities, skill potential and personality of migrants. In order to understand why people migrate, it would be necessary to enquire into the question why they do not, and under what conditions migration becomes stable or unstable.

SUBSISTENCE AND DEVELOPMENT MIGRATION

Migration has important economic consequences, both for the actual migrants and for the parental households and villages, depending on the type of migration. Broadly a distinction may be made between subsistence or distress migration and development migration. In the former, the people move out in search of work in order to survive. It includes a large number of construction workers, road building workers, and other unskilled and semi-skilled labourers. The economic gains of such migration are not sufficient to break the subsistence line. At best it might help migrants to buy food out of their savings to survive during months of unemployment. Secondly, migration under conditions of distress tends to be unstable, and this is so more because of conditions of employment rather than of any inherent love of the worker for his native village. Often workers are recruited on a contract basis only for a period of three to six months by the employers, especially in the category of small scale and medium scale industries. They do so in order to avoid payment of bonus and other benefits that they have to pay if they were to recruit the workers on a more permanent basis. Lack of strong unionisation of such workers and inadequate labour laws only convert potential stable labour force into a floating one.

Development migration, on the contrary, is characterised by a higher level of skills, training and education of the migrants. Such migrants qualify for more remunerative jobs. In many cases migrants will have to leave behind their wives, children and their parents. They send money home for the maintenance of their dependents, and this gives rise to a moneyorder economy resulting in developmental activities. The native family will be able to clear off loans and debts, build houses, eat good food and wear decent clothes. Besides this general improvement in the standard of life, in some cases, where the remittances are significant, as in the case of migrants from Punjab and Gujarat villages, the natal families invest in modern agricultural technology, small scale industries and establish educational institutions.

The development effects of another category of migrants who are engaged in trade, commerce and industry prove highly impressive. Many Marwaris who have migrated to towns and cities in different parts of India, save up substantial amounts of money which are not only reinvested in their business but also in philanthropic activities in home towns and villages, by building temples, hospitals, establishing educational trusts and institutions, and running eye operation camps.

OTHER CONSEQUENCES OF MIGRATION

Migration tends to be selective not only on the basis of age and sex but also on the basis of caste, religion, language, region, village and kinship ties. Normally, a single adult male moves in search of job to a town, secures one, and he in turn gets his friends and kinsfolk. In course of time a settlement based on language, kin, caste and region comes into being. Such settlements help create a situation of cultural pluralism, for the migrants from a particular region establish voluntary associations in a bid to recreate their home culture and also to fight for the basic necessities of urban life such as housing and education. They also provide security to the fresh immigrants and act as 'brokers'. Such favourable conditions of living in the place of destination attract more migrants on the one hand and make the migrant population more stable, on the other.

A substantial portion of the migrants live as squatters in slums developing cultural identity of their own and a community life based on it. Housing is cheap as it only means erecting another hut on the vacant plot. The area gets overcrowded and in the absence of any civic amenities slumming conditions get worse day-by-day. The city administration takes the view that the hutment dwellers are squatters, hence, it is not their responsibility to provide drainage, sewerage, water, electricity and garbage clearance services. However, it is necessary to take a sympathetic view of the hutment dwellers. In the absence of any programme on the part of the state to house the low-income group, the slums do provide an answer to their economic, social and cultural needs. Hence, development or clearance of slums becomes a necessary sequel to the immigration of the unskilled or semi-skilled workers.

Instead of thinking of solutions after the slums have come into existence, any sound planning should take into account measure of checking and controlling them. For instance, when the state establishes an industrial estate or a wholesale market, the housing of the labourers should form part of planning with all the urban infrastructure. Migration to metropolitan cities will have to be controlled and regulated at the very initial stage.

We should have enough information about the migrants: their identity in terms of employment, residence, places from which they have migrated, reasons for migration, local contacts, age, sex, skills, etc. This will help assess the state of unemployment among migrants with specific categories of skills, the directions of migration inflow, the demands made on housing, transport, communication and social welfare. A welfare state has to operate on these lines assuming all the responsibilities.

URBAN AREA DEVELOPMENT

An effective way of controlling indiscriminate migration is to plan develop the region, especially the metropolitan region, in terms of which there has already been a good deal of thinking. The industries need to be dispersed, adequate transport and communications will have to be provided. Even there is no escape from having a massive programme of establishing housing estates for the industrial workers and labourers, vendors and hawkers, and shack stall holders who follow the industries, markets and residential colonies. In the absence of a comprehensive plan the problem of indiscriminate migration and the consequent slum development will only get displaced but not solved.

The national capital region (Delhi) plan suggests dispersal of industries, administration and other activities and conceives of the settlement system in terms of seventeen growth centres. However, the problem is not so much the diversion of migrants by providing counter magnates and growth points but to handle the concomitant problems of new slums, new unauthorised colonies, new shack-shop complexes and new problems of crime, law and order. Hence, dispersal of industries and other economic activities alone will not lead to urban development. The central issue to me is to plan settlement of 60,000 migrants who pour into Delhi from rural areas every year, and who largely belong to the informal sector of the economy.

Another important aspect of urban development is the development of the inhabited areas of the villages in the metropolitan region. At present, in the name of not disturbing the villagers, the inhabited area is reduced to a slum-island in the midst of developed areas. This policy needs to be re-developed with all the urban infrastructure. In fact it should be considered as another means of providing compensation to the villages whose land will have been acquired for development purposes.

Further, the villages on the fringe of a metropolitan city or an industrial town are found to receive an influx of immigrant workers because of several advantages such as cheap housing, nearness to work and cheaper cost of living. Over a period of time the fringe villages become over-crowded and will be reduced to slums. Hence, the necessity of providing the urban infrastructure to prevent slumming conditions.

Any urban area development plan should consider city, towns and villages as functionally differentiated but inter-related. The villages with irrigational facilities should be encouraged to develop market gardening, dairy and poultry farming. Such villages not only provide the greenbelt for the metropolis but also act as a feeder belt supplying the commodities necessary for the city dwellers. Such developmental activities will also attract migrants who would have otherwise flocked to the city. Rural development is complementary to urban development; it helps dispersal of migrants.

Urban area development may take diverse patterns. The metropolitan area development may be conceived in terms of twin cities as in Bombay or satellite towns with the city at the centres as in Delhi and Madras. The conurbation should take the pattern which is best suited for the ecological and economic conditions of the region. Another pattern of regional development, in the absence of a metropolitan focus, is to provide multiple but interconnected foci. An aspect of the urban fringe development is the planning of the commuters' zone. People not only commute from villages and towns to the city but also from city to outskirts where industries are located. Thus, commuting is both centripetal and centrifugal. Efficient and quick mass transport is a pre-requisite in dispersal of settlements and avoiding congestion in the urban area.

In this context, development of smaller urban complexes including small and medium size towns needs to be stressed. For instance, Hospet-Bellary region in Karnataka has such a growth potential. Hospet has emerged as a mining town with manganese mines all around. Part of the region is canal irrigated and has become another rice bowl of Karnataka. Hospet is also a tourist centre with the ruins of Vijayanagar Empire and the Tungbhadra dam site. Bellary which is about forty miles from Hospet is the centre of trade and commerce, education and administration. With such a diversified but functionally related economic activities the area has all the potential for the development of small urban region.

Planning of small urban regions serves two important purposes. First, it helps the small towns, which are now decaying, grow. Secondly, it will divert the flow of migration to metropolitan centres thus bringing about balanced urban growth in the country.

REFERENCES

1. This is in line with the historical experience of developed countries and the ongoing experience of developing countries.
2. "The effect of changing economic conditions on levels and trends of mortality are not clear. There are examples of no mortality change under rapid economic progress, and substantial mortality decline under negligible or no economic growth." For citation of such instances, see: Simon Kuznets, "Demographic Aspects of Modern

Economic Growth", *World Population Conference*, Belgrade, August-September 1965 (Background paper: Session A-10). However, it is generally agreed in recent literature that the major factors in the developing countries are improvements in public health and adoption of medical technology, as opposed to improvements in economic conditions the levels of living. For example, see: George J. Stolnitz, "A Century of International Mortality Trends I and II", Population Studies, Vol. 9 (1955), pp. 24-25 and Vol. 10 (1065), pp. 17-42; also United Nations, *The Situation and Recent Trends of Mortality in the World*, Population Bulletin No. 6 (New York: United Nations, 1962).

3, 4. It can be hypothesized that an increase in agricultural output in a particular area may decrease mortality through improvements in level of nutrition and standard of living, attract immigration because of differential economic opportunity in favour of the area; and increase fertility directly through improved health condition, or decrease fertility indirectly through increases in the survival chances of infants and thus raising the average size of the family.

2

DRIFT IN POPULATION OF KARNATAKA

THE SIZE of India's population has been one of its distinguishing features. At the 1971 census, the population of India was 547,949,809 consisting of 283,936,614 males and 264,013,195 females. The population of Karnataka state, as on the reference date of the 1971 census, is 29,299,014 persons made up of 14,971,900 males and 14,327,114 females. Karnataka state thus contributes 5.35 per cent of the country's population. It is interesting to consider the population of this state in comparison with that of the other states and union territories.

Karnataka state is eighth both in area and population among the states in India. It accounts for 5.35 per cent of the country's population.

Distribution of population among the districts

The study of the distribution of population is important because this would indicate the way in which the population is arranged within the area available for exploitation and settlement. People use land for agriculture, forestry, mining, manufacturing, commerce and housing and, in so using the area available, they create patterns of distribution that reflect the adjustments with environment and resources. This spatial distribution of population can be viewed from different angles such as differentials densities of settlement, rural-urban concentrations, distribution with reference to natural resources, etc. However, the distribution of population can also be considered from the point of view of specific administrative units. A consideration of the distribution of population by districts and taluks gives a broad picture of the population profile of the state.

The average population of a district in the state is 1,542,053. Bengalore district has the highest population of 3,365,515, which is more than double the district average. The average district population is also exceeded by the districts of Belgaum (2,423,342), Dharwar (2,342,213), Mysore (2,077,238), Bijapur (1,985,591), South Kanara (1,939,315), Gulbarga (1,739,220) and Tumkur (1,627,721). Of these eight districts with populations higher than the average district population, the districts of Belgaum, Bijapur, Dharwar and Gulbarga are contiguous and lie in the Northern Maidan area of the state. Similarly, in the Southern part of the state, Bangalore, and Tumkur districts are contiguous.

The least populated district is Coorg with a population of 378,291, which is far below the average district population. The other districts with populations lower than that of the average district population are Chickmagalur (736,647), Bidar (824,059), North Kanara (849,105), Hassan (1,102,370), Bellary (1,122,686) Mandya (1,154,374), Shimoga (1,301,485), Chitradurga (1,397,456), Raichur (1,415,740), and Kolar (1,516,646). The population of the districts of Coorg, Chickmagalur, Bidar and North Kanara are less than one million. Coorg, Hassan, Mandya, Chickmagalur, Shimoga and North Kanara form one block, the districts being contiguous to each other. Similarly Bellary, Chitradurga and Raichur districts constitute one block.

The districts in the state are of different areas and their contributions both in terms of population and area to the population and area of the state vary widely. The proportion of population attributable to each district, the rank it takes in the population and area scales, with a comparison with 1961 are indicated in Table 2.1.

The districts of Bijapur, Gulbarga and Raichur which have the first three ranks on the area scale, have fairly lower ranks on the population scale. The largest district, Bijapur, has the fifth place in terms of population, while Gulbarga and Raichur have the seventh and tenth ranks respectively. The districts of

Bangalore, Belgaum, Dharwar, Mysore, South Kanara, Kolar, Mandya and Hassan have ranks on the population scale higher than what they have on the area scale. Tumkur, Bidar and Coorg districts have the same ranks both in terms of area and population. Coorg district occupies the lowest rank both in area and population.

It is interesting to notice that the districts occupy same ranks on the population-scale that they had in 1961 except in the case of Bellary and Mandya.

TABLE 2.1 : **Ranks of districts in terms of population and area**

Rank in population 1971	Name of district	Proportion of population of state in per cent	Proportion of area of state in per cent	Rank area	Rank in population in 1961
1	Bangalore	11.49	4.17	14	1
2	Belgaum	8.27	6.99	5	2
3	Dharwar	7.99	7.17	4	3
4	Mysore	7.09	6.23	6	4
5	Bijapur	6.78	8.89	1	5
6	South Kanara	6.62	4.40	12	6
7	Gulbarga	5.94	8.46	2	7
8	Tumkur	5.56	5.53	8	8
9	Kolar	5.18	4.29	13	9
10	Raichur	4.83	7.30	3	10
11	Chitradurga	4.77	5.66	7	11
12	Shimoga	4.44	5.50	9	12
13	Mandya	3.94	2.59	18	13
14	Bellary	3.83	5.16	11	14
15	Hassan	3.76	3.56	16	15
16	North Kanara	2.90	5.36	10	16
17	Bidar	2.81	2.84	17	17
18	Chickmagalur	2.51	3.76	15	18
19	Coorg	1.29	2.14	19	19

In 1961, Bellary had the 13th place and Mandya the 14th but in 1971, these districts have interchanged ranks, with Bellary now 14th and Mandya 13th.

The average area of a district in the state is 10,093 sq. km. of the 19 districts in the state, the ten districts of Belgaum, Bijapur, Chitradurga, Dharwar, Gulbarga, Mysore, North Kanara, Raichur, Shimoga and Tumkur have areas greater than the average area of a district, while the other nine districts have areas smaller than the average area of a district.

TABLE 2.2 : **Density of population of the districts**

Name of districts	Density of population (per sq. km.)					
	Total		Rural		Urban	
	1971	1961	1971	1961	1971	1961
Mysore state	153	123	118	97	2272	1717
Bangalore	421	310	193	153	7605	2400
Belgaum	181	149	148	124	1221	1295
Bellary	113	93	85	73	1185	1354
Bidar	151	123	131	108	2157	3200
Bijapur	116	98	95	81	729	773
Chickmagalur	102	82	87	70	2861	2056
Chitradurga	129	101	103	84	5071	3617
Coorg	92	78	79	68	1404	1585
Dharwar	170	142	122	107	1338	1368
Gulbarga	107	86	88	73	4738	3801
Hassan	162	129	141	115	3161	1837
Kolar	184	157	148	123	3175	2568
Mandya	233	185	204	167	2331	1590
Mysore	174	142	131	108	3815	2973
North Kanara	83	67	68	56	2048	2020
Raichur	101	78	86	68	2451	678
Shimoga	123	97	95	73	5752	1457
South Kanara	230	192	188	160	1897	2074
Tumkur	153	130	136	117	3127	2618

Density of population

The density of population is the number of persons per sq. km. The population of Mysore state as recorded at the 1971 census is 29,299,014 persons and its area is 191,773 sq. km. The density of population of the state is, therefore, 153 persons per sq. km. The density in 1961 was 123 persons per sq. km.

The density of population of the districts is indicated in Table 2.2. This statement indicates the density for all areas and for rural and urban areas separately. For comparison, the corresponding data for 1961 are also available.

The highest density is in Bengalore and the lowest in North Kanara district. The densities in the other districts range between these limits and there are considerable differences between district and district. The districts can be arranged on the basis of their densities above or below the state average as follows:

Districts with density above state average			Districts with density below state average		
		(State average 153)			
1	Bangalore	421	1	Bidar	151
2	Mandya	233	2	Chitradurga	129
3	South Kanara	230	3	Shimoga	123
4	Kolar	184	4	Bijapur	116
5	Belgaum	181	5	Bellary	113
6	Mysore	174	6	Gulbarga	107
7	Dharwar	170	7	Chickmagalur	102
8	Hassan	162	8	Raichur	101
			9	Coorg	92
			10	North Kanara	83

Tumkur district has a density equal to the state average of 153.

The rural density is highest in Mandya and least in North Kanara district. The districts can be arranged on the basis of rural densities being above or below the state average as follows:

Districts with rural density above state average			Districts with rural density below state average		
		(State average 118)			
1	Mandya	204	1	Chitradurga	103
2	Bangalore	193	2	Bijapur	95
3	South Kanara	188	3	Shimoga	95
4	Belgaum	148	4	Gulbarga	88
5	Kolar	148	5	Chickmagalur	87
6	Hassan	141	6	Raichur	86
7	Tumkur	136	7	Bellary	85
8	Bidar	131	8	Coorg	79
9	Mysore	131	9	North Kanara	68
10	Dharwar	122			

The highest urban density is in Bangalore district, the concentration being in Bangalore city, and the lowest urban density is in Bijapur district. The districts can be arranged on the basis of urban districts above or below the state average as follows:

Districts with urban densities above state average			Districts with urban densities below state average		
		(State average 2272)			
1	Bangalore	7605	1	Bidar	2157
2	Shimoga	5752	2	North Kanara	2048
3	Chitradurga	5071	3	South Kanara	1897
4	Gulbarga	4738	4	Coorg	1404
5	Mysore	3815	5	Dharwar	1338
6	Kolar	3175	6	Belgaum	1221
7	Hassan	3161	7	Bellary	1185
8	Tumkur	3127	8	Bijapur	729
9	Chickmagalur	2861			
10	Raichur	2451			
11	Mandya	2331			

The changes in densities between 1961 and 1971 are interesting. In 1961 the densities were below 100 in three groups of districts: the first group consisting of Bijapur, Gulbarga, Raichur, Bellary; the second group consisting of North Kanara, Shimoga, Chickmagalur; and the third group consisting of Coorg only. In 1971, the districts in the first group, namely, Bijapur, Gulbarga, Raichur and Bellary had moved upon the density scale and crossed 100 per sq. km. but of the districts in the second group only Shimoga and Chickmagalur crossed a density of 100, the increase in Shimoga being particularly high. North Kanara and Coorg districts, even in 1971, have densities below 100, though higher than those in 1961. Tumkur and Hassan districts, which had densities below 140 in 1961, have now crossed 150. Belgaum, Dharwar and Kolar districts, which were above the state average density in 1961 and also comparatively high density areas in 1961, continues to be so in 1971 also. The districts of Bangalore, Mandya and South Kanara were, in 1961, in the higher density ranges. They continue to be so in 1971 also. Bidar district has also increased in density.

In a few cases, there is an apparent fall in the urban densities in 1971 from that in 1961. This is due to methods of computation of density in the case of urban areas. (Urban areas include places constituted into municipalities, cantonments or other statutory areas where the areas of the built-up portions and total jurisdiction are clearly known, and also town panchayats or large villages declared as towns. In the case of town panchayats and large villages declared as towns, the population is usually concentrated in a gaothana or village core, the rest of the area being agricultural lands, but the area of the built-up portion is not known and the only area data available relate to the entire area of the village within its revenue limits.) The use of such large areas naturally lowers the density in such cases.

The total number of rural to urban migrants is 307,189 of which 161,286 or 52.50 per cent are males and 145,903 or 47.50 per cent are females. In terms of absolute number, the rural to urban migration within the state but outside the district of birth is much smaller than the rural to rural migration within the state but outside the district of birth. However, such a migration is one of the most important factors that influence urban population growth. In the case of the most of the districts, the male out-numbers females indicating that this type of migration is due to economic reasons. The largest proportion of rural to urban migrants consists of those who have moved from their villages and lived in towns for a duration of 1 to 5 years. The next large group are in the duration of 15 years and above. In the periods of duration of migration of 6-10 years, 11-15 years and 16 years and over, females exceed males, indicating the influence of migration consequent on marriage. In the shorter durations of less than one year and 1-5 years, males exceed females since the former migrate due to economic reasons.

Of the 307,189 migrants from rural areas of one district to urban areas of another district, 80,806 have moved into the urban areas of Bangalore district. This is clearly the result of the pull exerted by the Metropolitan area of Bangalore. The general pattern is that in the longer durations of such migration, the number of females exceeds that of the males, however, in Bangalore district, the number of males is greater than the number of females for all periods of duration of migration indicating the large influx into the Metropolitan Area of Bangalore of males.

For every 10,000 persons enumerated in the rural areas, 2,263 males and 5,214 females have been born outside the place of enumeration but within the district while 608 males and 919 females have been born in other districts of the state. Thus, those born within the same district far out-number those born in other districts. Migration is, therefore, more prominent within the same districts than from district to district. The migration within the districts is also largely from one rural area in the district to another. Out of the 2,263 males who are born within the district but outside the place of enumeration, 2,108 are from rural areas and 150 from urban areas. Among the 5,124 females who are born within the district but outside the place of enumeration, 4,966 belong to the rural areas and 240 are from the urban areas. The migration within the district is mostly rural to rural. The migration from the urban to the rural is only slight. This is understandable as the rural pull is less than the rural push. The rural to rural migration is mostly for social and other reasons, the economic reasons while no doubt present, are not so strong. The larger proportion of female migration is due to marriages only. Of those born outside the district, the larger proportions are again from the rural areas, the urban component being very small.

For every 10,000 persons enumerated in the urban areas 2,000 males and 2,836 females are born elsewhere in the district of enumeration, while 1,518 males and 1,469 females are born in other districts of the state. The difference in proportions between the males born elsewhere in the district and those born in other districts of the state is not very much indicating that the urban pull operates fairly uniformly. Of those born outside the place of enumeration but within the districts, the majority are from the rural areas of the district. Out of the 2,000 males, 1,416 are from the rural areas and 503 from the urban areas. Out of the 2,336 females, 1,674 are from the rural areas and 660 from the urban areas. Of those born in other districts of the state, the distribution between rural and urban areas is largely similar.

Coorg district has the highest percentage of inter-district immigration to the population of the district. However, in absolute numbers, this is less than that of Bangalore district. There is a net accretion to the population of the district, taking into consideration both in and out migration, in the districts of Bangalore, Chickmagalur, Chitradurga, Coorg, Dharwar, Gulbarga, Hassan, Mandya, North Kanara and Shimoga. In the other districts, migration has resulted in a net decrease in the total population of the district.

There is a constant movement of population between the various states of India. The total number of immigrants of Karnataka state from other states is 10,40,331 while the emigrants from this state to other state number 794,110. Thus, immigrants exceed emigrants by 246,221. Madras contributes the largest proportion of the immigrants with 38.13 per cent of the total immigrants being from that state. The next largest proportion of 27.98 per cent is from Andhra Pradesh followed by Maharashtra state with 16.27 per cent and Kerala with 13.19 per cent. Thus 95.57 per cent of the immigrants into Mysore state are from the neighbouring four states. The contribution from the Northern states is marginal, the largest being 1.24 per cent from Rajasthan.

The emigration from Karnataka to other states indicates that the largest proportion of emigrants goes to Maharashtra. Of the emigrants from the state, 58.96 per cent go to Maharashtra. The next largest proportion of 23.07 per cent go to Andhra Pradesh. Madras receives 11.17 per cent of the emigrants and Kerala only 2.69 per cent. Thus, 95.87 per cent of the emigrants go to the four neighbouring states. The proportion that emigrants North is very small.

The immigrants from Madras exceed the emigrants from Karnataka by 308,007. Those from Kerala exceed the emigrants to Kerala by 115,834 while in the case of Andhra Pradesh the difference is 107,904. In the case of Maharashtra, the emigrants from Karnataka exceed the immigrants from Maharashtra by 298,923. In the case of the states of Andhra Pradesh, Gujarat, Kerala, Madras, Punjab, Rajasthan and Uttar Pradesh, the number who come into Karnataka state exceed those that migrates from this state. In the case of the states of Assam, Bihar, Jammu and Kashmir, Madhya Pradesh, Maharashtra, Orissa and West Bengal, the numbers that leave Karnataka from these states exceed the number of those coming into the former from the latter.

Of the 10,40,331 migrants from other states into Karnataka state, 505,088 have migrated to the rural areas and 535,246 to the urban areas of the state; i.e., of the total migrants from other states, 48.55 per cent have migrated to the rural areas and 51.45 per cent to the urban areas of this state. Of the migrants from the various states, the greater proportion (66.83 per cent) of migrants in the case of Maharashtra move into the rural areas. Among the migrants from Madras, 64.68 per cent move into the urban areas. In the case of Andhra Pradesh, the greater proportion move into the rural areas. Among the migrants who come from the other states, and move into the rural areas of Karnataka state, the largest proportion is from Andhra Pradesh (34.11 per cent). The next largest proportion of migrants to the rural areas is from Madras (27.14 per cent). Kerala contributes 22.39 per cent and Maharashtra 14.47 per cent. In fact, 98.71 per cent of the migrants from other states who migrates to the rural areas of this state are from Andhra Pradesh, Kerala, Madras and Maharashtra. Among those from other states who migrates into the urban areas of Karnataka state, 47.93 per cent are from Madras, 22.19 per cent from Andhra Pradesh, 11.97 per cent from Kerala and 10.49 per cent from Maharashtra. Thus 92.58 per cent of the migrants from other states who migrate into the urban areas of Karnataka are from these four states.

Of the 172,280 migrants from Andhra Pradesh who migrate to the rural areas of Karnataka state, the larger number are found in the districts of Bellary, Bidar, Chitradurga, Gulbarga, Kolar, Raichur, Shimoga and Tumkur. In other words, 93.73 per cent of the migrants from Andhra Pradesh into the rural areas of Karnataka State are in these eight districts. The large numbers in the rural parts of Bellary and Raichur move in for agricultural work. This is true of the other districts also. Of the migrants from Andhra Pradesh to the urban areas in Karnataka, the larger proportions are in the districts of Bangalore, Bellary, Kolar, Raichur and Shimoga. The largest number is in Bangalore district.

Of those from Kerala who have migrated to the rural areas of this state, the larger proportions are in the districts of Chickmagalur, Coorg and South Kanara. They have migrated into these districts mainly as plantation labour. Of those from Kerala who have migrated to the urban areas of the state, the majority are found in the districts of Bangalore, Coorg, Shimoga and South Kanara.

Of those from Madras state who have migrated to rural areas of Karnataka state, the larger proportions are in the districts of Bangalore, Chickmagalur, Coorg, Hassan, Kolar, Mandya, Mysore and Shimoga. Of those from Madras who have migrated to the urban areas of Karnataka state, the larger proportions are found in the districts of Bangalore, Kolar, Mysore and Shimoga.

Of those from Maharashtra who have migrated to the rural

areas of Karnataka state, the larger proportions are in the districts of Belgaum, Bidar, Bijapur, Gulbarga and North Kanara. Of those from Maharashtra who have migrated to the urban areas of this state, the larger proportions are in the districts of Belgaum, Bijapur, Bangalore, Dharwar and Gulbarga.

Among those from the neighbouring states migrating to the urban areas of Karnataka state, the majority moves into Bangalore district from the state of Andhra Pradesh, Kerala and Madras. In the case of those from Maharashtra, the largest proportions of such migrants moves to the urban areas of Belgaum district. Among those who migrates to the rural areas of the State, those from Kerala are mainly in the plantation areas while those from Madras are distributed over the plantation areas and industrial areas. In the case of those from Andhra Pradesh, the majority of those who migrates to the rural areas of the state are in areas of agricultural activity.

Emigrants from Karnataka state to the other states in India is 794,110. These emigrants move either to the rural or urban areas of other states and their distribution is not uniform.

Of the total emigrants from the state, 40.05 per cent have migrated to the rural areas of other states while 59.95 per cent have migrated to the urban areas of other states. This follows the same characteristic as migration from other states into Karnataka where also the migration to urban areas exceeds that to the rural areas. Except in the case of the states of Andhra Pradesh, Jammu and Kashmir and Kerala where the number migrating from Karnataka to the rural areas of these states is greater, in all the other states, the migration from Karnataka to the urban areas exceeds that to the rural areas of the other states.

The emigrants from the rural areas of Karnataka are 477,918 to whom 318,117 of them migrate to the rural areas of other states, or 66.56 per cent of the rural emigrants from Karnataka migrate to the rural areas of other states. The rest, though from rural Karnataka, migrates to the urban areas of other states. Generally, the rural emigration is largely to rural areas of other states and urban emigration is largely to the urban areas of other states. However, in the case of Kerala, some of the urban emigrants from Karnataka migrates to the rural areas of Kerala. But the emigration from rural areas to urban areas of other states is also apparent.

The immigrants from outside the state account for 4.31 per cent of the males and 4.52 per cent of the females. There is a relatively greater proportion of males except in the districts of Belgaum, Bellary, Bidar, Bijapur, Chitradurga, Gulbarga, Kolar, Raichur and Tumkur. Except for Chitradurga district, the other districts mentioned are border districts and the relatively greater proportion of females in these districts among the immigrants is due to marriage migration from the neighbouring areas in the adjacent states. In the case of Chitradurga district which border Andhra Pradesh, as will be apparent, there is a fairly high proportion of migrants from Andhra Pradesh and since this group is likely to marry only from their own language group in their home state, the female proportion of immigrants is greater.

Bangalore district has a fairly high proportion of male immigration due to the employment opportunities available which would attract immigrants. The districts of Chickmagalur, Coorg and Shimoga have also high proportions of male immigrants because of the plantation labour that migrates from other states to these Malnad areas. Correspondingly, the proportion of female immigration into these districts is comparatively high due to marriage migration.

The actual population of the state is 23,586,772 consisting of 12,040,923 males and 11,545,849 females. If immigrants are excluded and emigrants are included, the result would be the natural population of the state or that population which the state would have had, had there been no migration at all. This natural population is 23,340,551 or 246,221 less than the actual population. Karnataka state receives more people than migrate from it. The actual sex ratio is 959 but the sex ratio on the basis of the natural population is 963. The difference is not significant. Thus, migration does not have any major influence on the sex ratio. The sex ratio of 1,027 in the case of immigrants from the adjacent states indicates that more females than males immigrates from the adjacent states. The sex ratio in the rural areas of such immigrants from the neighbouring states is 1,240, while for the urban areas it is 850. The number of females immigrating to the rural areas from the adjacent states exceeds the number of immigrating males while in the case of the urban areas the immigrating males exceed the females. The sex ratio is low in the case of immigrants from states other than the adjacent states.

The sex ratio of 1,203 is favourable to females in the case of emigrants from Karnataka state to the adjacent states. The emigration is largely due to marriage migration. The sex ratio in this case for the urban areas is, however, only 963 as against 1,386 for the rural areas. More emigration of females to the adjacent states occurs than of males, from the rural areas of Karnataka than from urban areas. The migration of females to the state other than the adjacent state is low. For every 1,000 males only 611 females emigrate to the state which are not adjacent to Karnataka state. The ratio is 687 for the urban areas and 457 for the rural areas. The emigration of females from the urban areas of the state to states other than adjacent states is greater than the emigration to these states of females from the rural areas of Karnataka.

The immigrants into Karnataka state from other states compared to the language returns for the numerically predominant languages of the respective states. Except in a few cases, the immigrants into the state are less in number than those in Karnataka who speak the predominant language of the state of origin. The difference in the number of migrants and the excess of speakers of the predominant language can be explained since the latter would include all those born in Karnataka state but talking the languages predominant in other states.

The immigration into the rural areas of Karnataka from the rural areas of the adjacent states is very much more prominent than that from the rural areas of states other than the adjacent states. Rural to rural migration is in a sense zonal. The number of rural female exceeds the immigrating males due to marriage migration. However, migration as such contributes only a small proportion to the rural population. Immigration into the rural areas is comparatively higher in the districts of Belgaum, Bellary, Chickmagalur, Coorg, Kolar, Shimoga and South Kanara. The proportion of rural immigrants from the rural areas of the other states to the rural population of the districts is comparatively higher in the districts of Belgaum, Bellary, Bidar, Chickmagalur, Coorg, Kolar, North Kanara and Shimoga.

Urban to urban migration in terms of absolute number is highest in Bangalore district. However, for the state as a whole immigrants from the urban areas of other states contribute less than five per cent of the total urban population of the state. As in the case of rural to rural immigration, in the case of urban to urban immigration also, the larger numbers are from the adjacent states. The proportion of such immigrants to the urban population is comparatively high in the districts of Bangalore, Bellary, Coorg and Shimoga.

The immigration from other states of India that marriage tends to bring in move female immigrants from the rural areas of other states into the urban areas of this state as the migration period increases. In case of migration from urban areas of other states of India into the urban areas of Karnataka state by duration, the conclusion drawn above regarding migration from rural areas of other states into the urban areas of Karnataka state hold good. For shorter duration of migration, males exceed females but as duration increases the numbers tend to equate (Table 2.[illegible]).

The immigrants under Category-I—cultivation—or II—agricultural labourers constitutes only small proportions of the total population in these industrial categories. The larger proportions of these immigrants who are cultivators are in the districts of Belgaum, Bellary, Bidar, Coorg, Gulbarga, Kolar and Tumkur. The largest proportion is in Kolar district. Of these immigrants in Category-II—as agricultural labourers, the larger proportions are in the districts of Belgaum, Bellary, Bidar, Chickmagalur, Chitradurga, Coorg, Gulbarga, Kolar, Mandya, Raichur, Shimoga and Tumkur. The highest proportion is in Coorg district. These districts are all areas of increased agricultural activity including irrigation into Karnataka state as percentages of the total, rural and urban population of Karnataka.

TABLE 2.3 : **Migrants of each sex for different durations of residents from rural areas of other states of India to urban areas of Karnataka state, 1961**

	Total migrants	1 year	1-5 years	6-10 years	11-15 years	16 years and over	Period not stated
Karnataka State							
P	278382	47343	83005	52172	32945	59840	3077
M	156155	30785	47710	27042	17250	31877	1491
F	122227	16558	35295	25130	15695	27963	1586
P	100.00	17.01	29.82	18.74	11.83	21.49	1.11
M	100.00	19.72	30.55	17.32	11.04	21.41	0.96
F	100.00	13.55	28.87	20.56	12.84	22.88	1.30
P	100.00	100.00	100.00	100.00	100.00	100.00	100.00
M	56.09	65.03	57.48	51.83	52.36	53.27	48.46
F	43.91	34.97	42.52	48.17	47.04	46.73	51.54

TABLE 2.4 : **Migrants from urban areas of other states of India to urban areas of Karnataka state, 1961**

	Total migrants	1 year	1-5 years	6-10 years	11-15 years	16 years and over	Period not stated
Karnataka State							
M	133138	23441	46175	23218	13606	24820	1878
F	116533	14622	38772	23490	13870	24810	1970

TABLE 2.5 : **Immigration from other states of India into the state, classified by sex, expressed by percentage of total, rural and urban population of the state, 1961**

Total/ Rural/ Urban	Population of state			Percentage of total immigrants from other states of India to actual population of state		
	Total	Male	Female	Total	Male	Female
Total	23536772	12040923	11545849	4.41	4.31	4.51
Rural	18320279	9287660	9032619	2.76	2.44	3.09
Urban	5266493	2753263	25132230	10.16	10.63	9.65

Immigrants from other states accounts for 4.41 per cent of the population of the state with 4.22 per cent from the adjacent states and only 0.19 per cent from the non-adjacent states. Immigration is largely from the neighbouring states. The proportions of male and female immigrants from the adjacent states are similar with a slightly higher proportion of females. But in the case of the non-adjacent states, the proportion of males exceeds that of females. In the case of the former, marriage migration accounts for the high proportion of female immigration while the latter would indicate that with increasing distances, marriage migration gets reduced. The proportion of migration from the adjacent states is very much more than from the states other than the adjacent ones. There is a greater proportion of migration to the urban areas than to the rural areas of Karnataka from the states which are not adjacent.

	Percentage of immigration from states adjacent to the state to actual population of state			Percentage of immigration from states other than those adjacent to state to actual population of state		
	Total	Male	Female	Total	Male	Female
T	4.22	4.07	4.36	0.19	0.24	0.15
R	2.72	2.40	3.06	0.04	0.04	0.03
U	9.41	9.73	9.06	0.75	0.90	0.59

Among those who have migrated into the state for less than one year, the males are far greater in number than the females. This is generally true in the migration period of 1-5 years and indicates that the males migrates in larger numbers for shorter durations due to economic reasons. As the duration increases, the number of females is almost equal to the number of males indicating utilisation, digging of wells and soil conservation works.

Category III includes those engaged in Mining and Quarrying, livestock, forestry, fishing, hunting and plantations, orchards and allied activities. The proportion of immigrants from other states to the total population engaged in this activity is 20.54 per cent. This is a fairly large proportion. The larger proportions are in the districts of Bellary (35.07 per cent), Chickmagalur (32.98 per cent), Coorg (42.60 per cent), Hassan (26.75 per cent), Kolar (36.04 per cent), North Kanara (10.58 per cent), Raichur (22.93 per cent) and Shimoga (19.10 per cent). The main activity in the districts of Chickmagalur, Coorg, Hassan, North Kanara and Shimoga would be in the plantations or forestry. In Bellary and Raichur it would be mining and quarrying. In Kolar district, mining would be the main activity for this category due to the existence of the Kolar Gold Mines.

The proportion in Category IV—Household Industry—is low being only 3.97 per cent for the state as a whole. It is, however, 33.69 per cent in Coorg district, and the main activity is manufacture of wood and wooden products. In Bangalore district, the immigrants engaged in household industry constitute 8.68 per cent of the proportion of the population of the district engaged in household industry. The main occupations include the production and rearing of livestock mainly for milk and animal power such as cows, goats, etc., and the rearing of silk worms and production of cocoons and raw silk. Cotton and silk weaving is also a prominent activity.

The proportion in Category V—manufacturing other than household industry, of immigrants to total population engaged in that category of industrial activity is 16.94 per cent. The major proportions are in Bangalore district (26.56 per cent), Bellary (22.84 per cent), Coorg (59.37 per cent), North Kanara

(27.35 per cent) and Shimoga (28.03 per cent). In Bangalore District, the main activity is in the manufacture of textile goods, stone dressing, electrical goods manufacturing and repair and in the air-craft factory and other central government factories. In Coorg, North Kanara and Shimoga districts, the manufacture of wood and wooden products is prevalent. In Shimoga district, many of the immigrants are engaged in the iron works there.

In Category VI—construction—the proportion of immigrants to the population engaged in that activity is 36.07 per cent. In Bangalore district the proportion is 31.62 per cent and the main economic activity is building construction and maintenance. In Bellary district it is 54.89 per cent and mainly engaged in the construction and maintenance of canals and bunds of the irrigation system in that district.

In 1971, out of the total population 99.89 per cent are born within the country and the rest are from outside India. Nearly 96 per cent of the total population in the state are born in the state. Of these, 68.74 per cent are born at the place of enumeration, 20.54 per cent are elsewhere in the district of enumeration and 6.66 per cent are in other districts of the state. Migrants from outside the state form a very small proportion of 3.95 per cent only and in that 3.70 per cent is accounted for by migrants from the neighbouring states of Tamil Nadu, Andhra Pradesh, Maharashtra and Kerala. Tables 2.6 and 2.7 give the distribution of population by place of birth as in 1971.

TABLE 2.6 : **Born in India, within the state of enumeration**

	Male	Female	Total
Born in the place of enumeration	11,495,864	8,644,514	20,140,378
Born elsewhere in the district of enumeration	2,065,842	3,953,558	6,019,410
Born in other districts of the state	832,717	1,118,741	1,951,458

It is observed that 93 per cent of the immigrants are from the neighbouring states of Tamil Nadu (29.81 per cent), Andhra Pradesh (29.71 per cent), Maharashtra (19.02 per cent), and Kerala (15.61 per cent). The proportion of migrants from other states is not significant except in the case of Rajasthan, which accounts for only 2.03 per cent.

Among the total immigrants, females exceed males in number from Andhra Pradesh, Maharashtra, and the union territories. The migration of females is obviously due to marriage and other socio-cultural factors. This also reflects the continued socio-cultural link of the northern districts of this state with the neighbouring state of Andhra Pradesh and Maharashtra. In the case of other states, male migrants exceed female.

It can be seen from Table 2.8 that Bangalore district has drawn the highest percentage (26.43 per cent) of migrants from other states and union territories in India whereas the least is in Mandya district (1.23 per cent). Next comes Belgaum district with 10.38 per cent of the total migrants from other states. The other districts are having less than 10 per cent of the migrants. Among males also Bangalore district with 30.57 per cent comes first followed by Belgaum (7.79 per cent) and South Kanara (7.19 per cent), the least being from Bidar (1.42 per cent). Among females Bangalore has absorbed the largest proportion with 22.53 per cent followed by Belgaum (12.80 per cent) and Kolar (7.55 per cent). The least is in Mandya district with one per cent of the total migrant population from outside the state.

About 62 per cent of the total male migrants move to rural areas (53 per cent from rural to rural and 7 per cent from urban to rural). On the other hand 23 per cent (13 per cent from rural to urban, 10 per cent from urban to urban) of the female migrants move to urban areas as against 38 per cent (20 per cent rural to urban, 18 per cent urban to urban) for males. Here it is observed that the movement of males is more than that of females to urban areas where more job opportunities and educational facilities are available. Females move mainly in connection with family rather than for employment. If we compare

TABLE 2.7 : **Number of inter-state immigrants from other states and union territories and proportion they constitute in the total immigrant population of the Karnataka state, 1971**

Birth place State/Union territory	Immigrants from other states and union territories		
	Persons	Male	Female
Total immigrants from other states	1,157,813 (100.00)	561,867 (100.00)	595,946 (100.00)
Andhra Pradesh	337,720 (29.17)	143,990 (25.63)	193,730 (32.50)
Assam	650 (0.06)	470 (0.80)	180 (0.03)
Bihar	2,845 (0.25)	2,140 (0.38)	705 (0.13)
Gujarat	8,460 (0.74)	4,845 (0.86)	3,615 (0.61)
Haryana	1,810 (0.15)	1,475 (0.26)	335 (0.05)
Himachal Pradesh	1,175 (0.10)	780 (0.14)	395 (0.05)
Jammu and Kashmir	655 (0.06)	500 (0.08)	155 (0.03)
Kerala	180,764 (15.61)	115,978 (20.65)	64,786 (10.87)
Madhya Pradesh	2,500 (0.21)	1,315 (0.24)	1,185 (0.20)
Maharashtra	220,160 (19.02)	73,475 (13.08)	146,685 (24.62)
Manipur	100 N	70 N	30 N
Meghalaya	10 N	5 N	5 N
Nagaland	55 N	25 N	30 N
Orissa	735 (0.06)	520 (0.09)	215 (0.04)
Punjab	4575 (0.39)	3,120 (0.56)	1,455 (0.25)

Rajasthan	23,465	(2.03)	15,350	(2.74)	8,115	(1.36)
Sikkim	10	N	10	N	—	—
Tamil Nadu	344,954	(29.81)	182,349	(32.46)	162,605	(27.29)
Tripura	40	N	30	N	10	N
Uttar Pradesh	8,910	(0.76)	6,065	(1.08)	2,845	(0.48)
West Bengal	4,115	(0.36)	2,500	(0.45)	1,615	(0.27)
Union Territories	14,105	(1.22)	6,855	(1.22)	7,250	(1.22)

Note: 1. 'N'—Negligible.

2. Figures within brackets indicate percentage.

TABLE 2.8 : **Percentage distribution among districts of Karnataka state to total of immigrants from other states in India, 1971**

State/District	Person	Male	Female
Bangalore	26.43	30.57	22.53
Belgaum	10.38	7.79	12.80
Bellary	6.34	5.94	6.72
Bidar	3.38	1.42	5.25
Bijapur	3.50	2.73	4.23
Chickmagalur	2.65	3.23	2.10
Chitradurga	2.93	2.73	3.12
Coorg	3.82	5.04	2.68
Dharwar	2.53	2.87	2.20
Gulbarga	4.84	3.16	6.43
Hassan	1.68	2.13	1.26
Kolar	6.20	4.77	7.55
Mandya	1.23	1.46	1.00
Mysore	4.77	5.53	4.05
North Kanara	2.07	2.44	1.71
Raichur	4.13	4.53	3.76
Shimoga	3.49	4.18	2.84
South Kanara	6.33	7.19	5.50
Tumkur	3.30	2.29	4.27
Karnataka State	100.00	100.00	100.00

this movement within rural areas females move less from urban to rural than males (9.53 per cent males and 7.36 per cent females). The reason for this higher mobility among males may be seasonal migrations of males for contract jobs. Also male students may be moving to urban areas for education and on completion, returning home.

3

PATTERNS OF CHILD MIGRATION

Mobility of India's population has gradually been growing particularly since independence. In the context of a predominantly agricultural economy and a consistently fast growing population the small and declining size of agricultural land holdings has been basic to the process of out-migration. The zeal to improve the standard of living has been another vital consideration which is vivid in increasing migration from small towns to big cities and the movement of landless agricultural labourers (mostly belonging to scheduled castes) from rural areas to urban places. The proximity to urban-industrial concentrations and major construction sites was a strong pull factor.[1] Migration can be a disturbing influence on educational attainment of children. Among all the migrant children in the cities, the plight of the children of migrant construction workers are the most miserable as they move from site to site in search of jobs.

This section has been prepared from the available data on child migrants and child migrant labour which is given in Indian Censuses of 1961 and 1971. It examines the amount and extent of state-wise child-migrants, child migrant labour in the cities of India. It analyses the nature of employment patterns of migrant children in the cities. The data for this is taken from DIV migration tables of 1961 census. Here the migrants are identified from the information of place of birth. This information fails to measure the intermediate and multiple movements. This error may not be very serious in the case of child migrants as many of them might not have made more than one movement. However, some of them, especially, those who made short distance movements might have identified as migrants just because of the custom prevalent in the country for a woman to return to her father's household for deliveries. This section also analyses data on child migrants in Bangalore city, Greater Bombay, Karnataka, for this purpose data regarding place of last residence in 1971 census are utilized. The information on place of last residence was collected in respect of every person irrespective of his place of birth if he had another place of normal residence before he came to the present place where he was enumerated. Therefore, migrants are all persons who have migrated at any time, thus it includes return migrants. Besides, this information reflects direct movement between places.

Extent of child migrants in the cities of various states

State-wise child migration rates in the cities according to the 1961 census are given in Table 3.1 (Few of the town groups are also included in these data). Out of about 13.4 million child population in these cities about 3 million (22.8 per cent) were recorded as migrants. The two states which had high child migration rates were Assam (54.5 per cent) and Orissa (37.4 per cent) and the two states with low rates were Jammu and Kashmir (8 per cent) and Kerala (12.8 per cent). In the case of total migrants, if Delhi is excluded, the states which recorded high rates of migration were Assam (61.2 per cent) and Punjab (58.3 per cent) and the low rates were in Jammu and Kashmir and Kerala. The extent of child migrants and the total migrants are positively associated. The rank correlation coefficient between these is +0.79 which is statistically significant at one per cent level. Surprisingly it is found that the child migration rate is negatively associated with the sex ratio of the total stream. Thus the data goes against the impression that the stream with more females have more children.

Corresponding to every 100 migrants aged 15 and above enumerated in the cities there were 22 child migrants. In Orissa and Assam, the ratio of child migrants were high, the lowest was in Maharashtra. If the ratio of young male migrants and female migrants to male aged 15 and above can be taken as a measure of family migration, around 1.1 dependent persons accompany or follow the male migrants aged 15 and above, in the cities of India. This measure indicates that family migration is low in the cities of Assam, Maharashtra and West Bengal and high in all the South Indian cities, Cuttack city and in the cities of Rajasthan.

Child labour in the cities of various states

Child labour is a social evil which cannot be easily abolished. As long as poverty exists it will persist in some form or another. Another reason for child labour is that is attractive to employers because children work for lower wages than adults and also because they do not have statutory rights and previleges. At the time of industrial revolution, there had been widespread exploitation of child lobour in the western countries. In India, child labour is banned in many of the organised sectors. Due to these legal restrictions, many children due to practical necessity of work are forced to work in the unorganised sector, where working conditions are atrocious. They are often exploited. Out of 3 million child migrants in these cities, about 98 thousand (3.2 per cent) were workers. Sex-wise work participation ratio was 4.8 per cent for males and 1.4 per cent for females. Between the states there are great variations. The work participation ratio among male children was observed in Jammu and Kashmir (8.7 per cent) and lowest in Gujarat (2.4 per cent). Among females the highest work participation ratio was in Kerala (7.5 per cent) and lowest in Orissa (0.1 per cent). Kerala is the only state where WPR of girls was greater than boys. It is surprising that the highest work participation ratio among young migrant girls was in the same state where child labour is the lowest and the educational level of women is the highest. In many socio-demographic characteristics Kerala is different from rest of India. Work participation ratio of child migrants in this state is also different from the rest. Poor families in Kerala do not feel relevant to send boys as well as girls for work away from their home. Some of the difference in the work participation ratio of children by state could be due to the difference in

TABLE 3.1 : **State-wise data regarding migration rate among total population, sex ratio of total migrants, young migrants as percentage of total migrants aged 15 and above, ratio of young migrants and female migrants aged 15 and above to total male migrants aged 15 and above, WPR among young migrant, young migrant workers as percentage of young workers to the cities of various states, 1961**

	Migration Rate		Sex ratio of migrants females/males	Young migrants / Total migrants aged 15 and above (Percentage)	Young male migrants and total female migrants / male migrants age 15+	WPR of young migrants		Young migrant workers as percentage of young workers		Percentage of migrant working boys to young migrant workers
	Total population	Children				M	F	M	F	
Andhra Pradesh (11)*	36.8	21.1	1009	29.4	1.5	6.9	3.0	28.3	39.7	66.7
Assam (1)	61.2	54.5	396	38.2	0.7	4.8	0.7	88.7	54.7	87.1
Bihar (7)	43.9	21.0	795	23.0	1.2	7.4	1.4	48.8	32.3	85.1
Gujarat (6)	44.3	21.4	825	23.7	1.2	2.4	0.5	36.6	26.2	85.3
Jammu and Kashmir (2)	19.8	8.0	938	20.6	1.3	8.7	0.2	13.7	2.5	98.2
Kerala (5)	30.0	12.8	975	20.3	1.4	6.5	7.5	46·3	52.4	46.5
Madhya Pradesh (8)	48.7	22.0	814	21.5	1.2	3.5	1.8	35.4	40.1	69.1

Tamil Nadu (9)	36.7	16.6	907	20.1	1.3	5.4	2.5	28.0	31.3	69·6
Maharashtra (12)	58.3	27.1	652	19.1	0.9	5.4	2.0	62.0	47.3	75.4
Karnataka (6)	38.9	18.8	901	24.0	1.3	7.2	2.9	30.0	31.7	70.8
Orissa (1)	37.2	37.4	755	51.5	1.6	5.1	0.1	46.9	3.9	98.7
Punjab (5)	58.3	24.3	789	19.7	1.1	6.1	0.4	63.6	41.8	94.3
Rajasthan (6)	36.5	20.4	899	29.9	1.4	3.6	0.8	26.8	28.3	79.0
Uttar Pradesh (17)	37.8	17.6	831	23.0	1.1	5.4	0.8	26.6	35.2	88.9
West Bengal (12)	54.6	30.5	495	21.6	0.8	3.0	0.3	43·3	47.1	93.8
D.M.C. and New Delhi (2)	64.8	32.5	756	25.0	1.2	3.9	0.5	67.3	59.5	89.0
ALL INDIA (109)	46.9	22.8	735	22.3	1.1	4.8	1.4	38.5	38.7	78.6

Source: 1. Census of India, 1961, Vol. I, Part II-C (iii), India, Migration Tables (1)-IV.

2. Census of India, 1961, Vol. I, Part II-B (i), India, General Economic Tables (B-II).

* The figures inside the brackets are the number of cities.

the age composition within the age group 0-14. Standardization is not possible as the age composition is not known.

In the cities of India, nearly 79 per cent of the child workers were boys. In Orissa and Jammu and Kashmir almost all the workers were boys. Kerala is the only state where migrants female workers out-numbered male workers. It may be noted that in the cities of Kerala the participation rate of non-migrant female children was also slightly higher than the rate of male children. This phenomenon observed in Kerala may be due to the limited type of jobs available for children.

Nearly 39 per cent of the child workers in the cities were migrants. In Assam 82 per cent of the child workers were migrants while the percentage of Jammu and Kashmir was only 13 per cent. If the workers among male children are only considered it has been observed that 89 per cent of the workers in Assam, 67 per cent in Delhi and 64 per cent in Punjab were migrants. It has been further observed that the proportion of migrants among the child labour is directly associated with the child migration rate. The rank correlation between the child migration rate and the proportion of migrants among the child workers is 0.77 which is statistically significant at one per cent level. In the case of males, it is observed that in the cities of Kerala, Bihar, Punjab, Delhi, Maharashtra and Tamil Nadu, the ranks of child migration rate exceeded the ranks of migrants among child labour. Maximum difference is registered for Kerala. This indicates that compared to other cities to the cities of these states male children would be migrating for employments. In these cities WPR of male children were also high. Delhi was an exception. The case of Jammu and Kashmir was peculiar because here both the child migration rate as well as the migrants among child labour were the lowest but the WPR of migrant male children was the highest. In Jammu and Kashmir the WPR of non-migrant male children was also the highest. This could be due to the very low literacy level of the people in this state.

Occupational composition of working migrant children in the cities

Distribution of child workers in each of the states by occupational divisions are given in Table 3.2 and Table 3.3. Out of 77 thousand child migrant workers about 18 thousand were working in Maharashtra. Nearly 64 per cent of the working males were working in Maharashtra, Uttar Pradesh, West Bengal, Andhra Pradesh and Delhi. More than 9 in 10 of migrant males were occupied in three occupational divisions, namely, 'Craftsmen and Labourers' (43.5 per cent), 'Services' (36.9 per cent) and 'Sales' (10.9 per cent). The type of work done by male children in the cities of different states is shown in Table 3.2. In Orissa (Cuttack city) about 53 per cent of the migrant boys were employed in 'Sales' while in Kerala only 3.9 per cent were engaged in this division. In contrast 82 per cent of the child workers in cities of Kerala were employed in 'services'.

Maximum differentials with respect to occupational distribution, from the all-India pattern is observed for states Kerala and Orissa which is revealed by the summary measure of the coefficient of dissimilarity (46.7 and 43.0 respectively). The minimum measure of co-efficient of dissimilarity is observed for Punjab.

Out of total seventy-five occupational groups, only twelve were relevant for migrant male children. Nearly 60 per cent of the workers were employed in five occupational divisions, namely: (1) housekeepers, cooks, maids, and related workers (24.8 per cent); (2) labourers not elsewhere classified (13.7 per cent); (3) Waiters, bar-tenders and related workers (7.3 per cent); (4) Salesmen, shop assistants and related workers (7.1 per cent); (5) Spinners, weavers, knitters, dyers and related workers, (6.5 per cent). Thus good number of these boys were employed by the affluent families and small hotels. Cuttack is the only city which did not employ migrant boys as domestic help and in small hotels while in cities of Kerala 77 per cent of the working boys were employed in this group. More than half of the working boys in Cuttack city were employed as 'Salesmen shop assistants and related workers'. When a search is made to find out the probable reasons for this difference, it has been observed that the occupational distribution of migrants in the cities of

TABLE 3.2 : **Percentage distribution of migrant working children in**

Occupational divisions	Males							
	Andhra Pradesh	Assam	Bihar	Gujarat	Jammu and Kashmir	Karnataka	Kerala	Madhya Pradesh
Cultivators	0.7	—	0.7	0.2	0.2	3.9	0.1	1.5
Agricultural Labourers	1.8	—	0.6	0.4	0.2	2.9	—	1.0
Professional	0.8	—	0.7	0.5	—	1.3	0.4	0.5
Administrative	0.2	—	0.3	0.5	—	0.2	0·1	0.1
Clerical	3.3	0.5	1.0	1.7	1.5	2.5	0.5	0.8
Sales	9.3	5.0	6.4	12.3	5.6	8.0	3.9	10.9
Farmers	4.7	—	3.0	4.2	1.8	3.9	0.4	3.8
Miners	0.3	—	—	—	—	0.1	—	0.7
Transport	1.0	1.2	0.2	2.6	0.2	0.6	2.2	0.5
Craftsmen and Labourers	58.7	64.8	23.0	35.9	22.5	49.8	10.1	57.5
Services	19.2	28.3	62.6	41.7	68.0	26.2	82.2	22.6
Unclassified	—	0.2	1.5	—	—	0.6	0.1	0.1
Total	100.0	100.0	100.0	100.0	100.0	100.0	100.0	100.0
No. of cases	6855	400	4137	2382	594	5270	1137	2904
Co-efficient of dissimilarity	20.52	21.74	27.65	10.00	31.11	14.27	46.74	17.34

Source: Census of India, 1961, Vol. I, Part II-C (iii), India, Migration

the cities by occupational divisions and state of enumeration, 1961

Maharashtra	Orissa	Punjab	Rajasthan	Tamil Nadu	Uttar Pradesh	West Bengal	Delhi	India
0.2	—	0.8	0.4	0.1	0.3	0.1	0.3	0.6
0.8	—	0.8	0.7	0.4	0.6	0.1	0.2	0.8
0.9	1.3	0.4	2.6	0.3	3.2	1.1	0.8	1.2
0.7	—	0.7	2.4	0.4	1.0	0.2	1.1	0.6
1.4	1.3	0.5	3.1	1.9	3.5	1.9	1.0	1.9
12.2	53.0	10.1	12.8	15.6	10.0	14.9	5.2	10.9
1.6	—	1.3	1.7	2.4	1.6	0.7	0.8	2.1
0.1	—	—	0.3	—	—	—	0.5	0.1
0.6	—	0.5	2.5	0.8	1.0	0.4	0.5	0.8
36.2	44.4	45.9	53.1	52.8	54.1	36.0	38.0	43.5
45.1	—	39.0	19.1	25.2	23.4	43.1	51.4	36.9
0.2	—	—	1.3	0.1	1.3	1.5	0.2	0.6
100.0	100.0	100.0	100.0	100.0	100.0	100.0	100.0	100.0
18045	525	3369	1662	5774	10473	7712	6141	77380
9.56	43.07	4.38	18.66	14.23	15.59	11.12	15.42	

Tables (D-IV).

TABLE 3.3 : **Percentage distribution of migrant working children enumeration, 1961**

Occupational division	Females State of Enumeration Andhra Pradesh	Assam	Bihar	Gujarat	Jammu and Kashmir	Karnataka	Kerala	Madhya Pradesh
Cultivators	1.5	—	2.1	2.9	—	8.8	—	4.1
Agricultural Labourers	4.8	—	3.9	1.2	—	2.3	0.1	1.5
Professional	0.9	—	1.8	2.0	9.1	0.5	0.2	0.4
Administrative	0.1	—	0.1	—	—	—	—	—
Clerical	0.3	—	0.5	0.2	—	0.5	—	0.1
Sales	3.0	—	2.6	2.2	—	1.1	—	1.2
Farmers	0.8	3.4	1.7	9.3	—	3.1	—	2.0
Miners	0.9	—	—	0.7	—	0.2	—	1.1
Transport	—	—	—	2.5	—	—	—	0.1
Craftsmen and Labourers	48.2	6.8	41.4	49.5	18.2	48.3	2.8	72.7
Services	39.4	89.8	45.8	29.5	72.7	34.8	96.9	16.8
Unclassified	0.1	—	0.1	—	—	0.4	—	—
Total	100.0	100.0	100.0	100.0	100.0	100.0	100.0	100.0
No. of workers	3431	(59)	725	410	11	2175	1307	1296
Co-efficient of dissimilarity	7.94	46.85*	3.38	16.95	35.12*	12.90	52.08	32.82

in the cities by occupational divisions and state of

Maharashtra	Orissa	Punjab	Rajasthan	Tamil Nadu	Uttar Pradesh	West Bengal	Delhi	India
0.9	—	—	2.9	0.2	2.0	—	2.9	2.1
2.8	—	2.0	4.1	0.9	0.8	0.2	3.2	2.4
2.0	—	1.5	6.1	0.7	7.6	7.1	1.9	1.9
0.2	—	1.0	0.7	0.1	—	—	—	0.1
0.4	—	—	0.9	0.1	0.4	0.4	—	0.3
2.2	100.00	3.0	2.5	1.3	2.4	3.5	3.2	2.0
0.5	—	2.4	5.4	0.7	4.6	0.4	1.2	1.5
0.1	—	—	0.9	—	—	—	2.6	0.4
0.1	—	—	0.2	0.1	—	—	—	0.1
43.9	—	54.2	55.3	37.8	56.0	35.1	37.7	44.1
46.9	—	35.9	21.0	58.1	25.0	51.7	46.4	44.9
—	—	—	—	—	1.2	1.6	0.9	0.2
100.0	100.0	100.0	100.0	100.0	100.0	100.0	100.0	100.0
5873	7	203	443	2523	1307	510	758	1038
2.86	97.98*	12.85	21.08	13.31	22.25	15.07	7.21	

Kerala were different from that in Cuttack city. In cities of Kerala nearly 12 per cent of the migrants were employed in professional occupations against 3 per cent in Cuttack city. Thus the migrants in cities of Kerala could afford to have domestic help. Besides, WPR among migrant females in Kerala were almost double that in Cuttack city. Nearly 10 per cent of the workers in Cuttack city were employed in household industry, while in the cities of Kerala only 3.4 per cent were thus employed. Majority of child migrants in Cuttack city could get jobs in the sales of household manufactured goods while those in Kerala could get employed in households as domestic help or in small hotels or restaurants.

Out of 21 thousand migrant working girls 28 per cent were working in Maharashtra and 16 per cent were working in Andhra Pradesh. If we include Tamil Nadu and Karnataka also in these four states, two-thirds of the girls were working. In the case of female workers, nearly 9 out of 10 were employed in the two occupational divisions (1) 'services' (44.9 per cent), and (2) 'Craftsmen and labourers' (44.1 per cent). About two-thirds of the working girls were employed in the three occupational categories: (1) housekeepers, cooks, maids, and related workers (40.6 per cent); (2) 'Labourers not elsewhere classified' (14.6 per cent); and (3) 'Spinners, weavers, knitters, dyers and related workers' (11.3 per cent). Thus, among girls at least 4 in 10 were employed by the affluent families. In Kerala almost all the migrant female workers were working as housekeepers, cooks, maids and related workers. The lowest proportion in this category was observed in Uttar Pradesh.

The literacy level of migrant workers in Gujarat and Punjab were higher than the rest. The lowest literacy level was observed for the migrant workers in Jammu and Kashmir and Orissa (Table 3.4). In all the cities of the states, the literacy level of young migrant workers were lower than the young migrants. The magnitude of the difference in the literacy level of the migrants and that of the workers could have been measured in a better way, if the literacy level of persons aged 5-14 were compared. Nevertheless, this table indicates that the child migrant workers had a lower literacy than the child migrants.

On the whole about eleven per cent of the male workers and nearly 5 per cent of the female workers had an educational level of primary and above. Migrant working children were from families of lower socio-economic status.

TABLE 3.4 : Percentage primary and above among young migrants and young migrant workers in the cities of each of the states in India, 1961

State of Enumeration	Young migrants		Young migrant workers	
	Males	Females	Males	Females
Andhra Pradesh	25.4	19.4	13.0	3.4
Assam	32.9	18.7	10.5	—
Bihar	20.5	13.0	2.8	1.5
Gujarat	37.1	34.3	25.3	12.2
Jammu and Kashmir	10.4	7.6	0.8	—
Karnataka	24.2	19.5	9.6	4.2
Kerala	22.9	21.4	10.6	6.3
Madhya Pradesh	11.0	8.9	6.3	1.2
Maharashtra	23.8	19.7	14.8	6.0
Orissa	22.3	14.8	1.1	—
Punjab	30.5	27.6	23.2	15.3
Rajasthan	6.9	4.4	1.1	0.9
Tamil Nadu	29.1	24.4	18.4	7.2
Uttar Pradesh	21.3	12.9	6.6	1.3
West Bengal	19.7	16.9	6.0	8.6
Delhi	18.3	17.7	8.3	2.9
All India	22.6	18.4	11.2	4.8

Child migrants and child labour in cities

According to 1961 census in Greater Bombay, out of 400,754 child migrants, 16,643 (4.2 per cent) were working and 78 per cent of these workers were males. According to 1961 census in Bangalore city, out of 83,869 child migrants, 4,604 (5.49 per cent) were working and 74 per cent of these workers were males.

Data regarding child migrant workers are not directly available in 1971 census. Only the combined figure of migrant workers aged 0-14 and 60 and above is available. The migrant workers aged 60 and above can be estimated from the total workers aged 60 and above assuming that the ratio of work participation rate of migrants to total workers by age group is same in 1961 and 1971. The estimated child workers in Bangalore city is 45.02 (4.96 per cent). According to this estimate the child migrant labour is nearly 74 per cent of the child labour in Bangalore city. The slight decline observed in WPR in Bangalore city in 1971 could be due to the change in the concept of worker at the two censuses. Students doing secondary work being excluded in 1971 census could be very high.

It has been found that the extent of child migrants is positively associated with the extent of total migrants in the cities of India. Nearly 23 per cent of the children in the cities were recorded as migrants. Corresponding to every hundred migrants aged 15 and above enumerated in the cities of India there were 22 child migrants. Between the states the extent of child migration to the cities varied. The highest child migration rate was in Assam (Gouhati city 55 per cent) and lowest was in Jammu and Kashmir (8 per cent). Workers constituted 3.2 per cent of the child migrants in the cities. Nearly 8 in 10 of the migrant child workers were males. Only in the cities of Kerala, female migrant child workers out-numbered male workers and the highest work participation among female children was also in Kerala.

Nearly 39 per cent of the child workers in the cities were migrants. It ranged from 82 per cent in Assam to 13 per cent in Jammu and Kashmir. The general observation was that wherever the total migration was high the proportion of migrant child labour was also high. Migrant children were employed only in certain type of jobs mainly because of their age, training, suitability and also because child labour is cheap. More than 9 in 10 migrant male children were occupied in four occupational divisions—namely 'Craftsmen and labourers' (43.5 per cent), services (36.9 per cent), and sales (10.9 per cent). Nearly 25 per cent of male children and 41 per cent of female children were employed in the single occupational category 'housekeepers, cooks, maids and related workers'. Therefore, the maximum proportion of migrant children were employed by the affluent families and small hotels or restaurants. The distribution of these young migrant workers by occupational categories varied between states. Higher incidence of migrant child labour may be due to various reasons like the extent of general migration, availability of jobs, socio-economic level of the population of the sending areas, etc. The cause of child labour and the conditions under which they work are not known from census data. Economic compulsion is stated as the major reason for the children to join the labour force by some of the special studies.[2] The type of work in which they are engaged involves long hours of respective work without proper holidays and the remuneration especially as domestic help or in hotels and restaurants are very low. Type of migrations of children in states show that majority of rural children made short distance migrations, while migrant children in the urban areas mostly made long distance migrations. The type of migration made by children was very much also with that of the orders. Even though the child migration was mostly due to sequential reasons, extent of child migration and especially the working migrants depends on various other factors. This requires a special study.

REFERENCES

1. G.S. Gosal and G. Krishna, "Patterns of Internal Migration in India" in *People on Move Studies on Internal Migration*, edited by Leszek, A. Kosinski and R. Mannsell, Methuen Co. Ltd., London, 1975.
2. Musafar Singh and others, *Working Children in Bombay—A Study*, National Institute of Public Cooperation and Child Development, New Delhi, 1978.

4

THE RURAL URBAN INTERNAL MIGRATION

Its Socio-Economic Correlates

STUDIES starting from Revenstein (1885 and 1889) have tried to account for the migration differences through certain chosen variables. Zipf (1946) proposed that number of migrants is directly proportional to distance. For Stouffer (1940), it is availability of opportunities at destination which account for migration. Prior migration is considered to be important by Greenwood (1969). Combining Zipf and Greenwood's propositions and taking into account both distance and previous migration, Terver and Mcleod (1973) were successful in predicting inter-state migration in U.S.A. Significant correlations have also been found between a current and previous migration in India (Singh and Yadav 1974). Stouffer's availability of opportunities is in a way related to prior migration for it is mostly through previous migrants that this reaches potential migrant, and Zipf's geographic distance is countered by psychological (Burford 1962) and social distance depending on presence or absence of Kin at places of destination. A comprehensive econometric model includes all these variables to predict the volume of migration.

$$Mij = f\,(Yij : UiUj;\ Zizj;\ Dij,\ Cij)$$

Where i= **Place of origin, and**

j= Place of destination;
Mij= Variables explaining migration;
Y= Income levels;
U= Unemployment rates;
Z= Degree of Urbanisation;
Dij= Distance between place of origin and place of destination;
Cij= Friends and relatives in place of destination (World Bank Staff Working Paper 1975).

Density of population, agricultural productivity are correlated with migration, positively in the case of former and negatively in case of latter (Dasgupta and Laishley 1975). A tendency for better educated to be more mobile is often reported (Thomas 1938, Caldwell 1969). When certain geographic/administrative units are considered, how far the differential rate of migration are explained by these variables? The basic difficulty in this issue is the unit of consideration. If the unit is too small or too large the variables explain everything or nothing respectively. The districts in Karnataka are taken as units for comparison here and 1960-61 and 1970-71 data from published reports are analysed.

How far the variables viz. (1) density of population; (2) percentage of literates; (3) births per 100 in the year 1960 and 1970; (4) percentage of households in agricultural occupation; (5) percentage of area sown twice to net area sown; (6) foodgrains production per acre in kg.; (7) percentage of populations dependent on agricultural wages for livelihood, are related to the proportion of non-migrants in the district and different types of migrations namely: rural-rural, rural-urban, urban-rural and urban-urban is bested.

Migration in Karnataka

According to 1961 census, 22.33 per cent (11.67 per cent males; 10.66 per cent females) of Karnataka population is urban as against to 24.31 per cent (12.71 per cent males; 11.60 per cent females) of Karnataka in 1971 census is urban. Similarly, 77.67

per cent (39.38 per cent males; 38.29 per cent females) is rural in 1961; as against to that of 1971 census 75.69 per cent (38.39 per cent males; 37.30 per cent females) is rural. As could be seen from Table 4.1, 69-75 per cent of rural and 60.97 per cent of urban population are born and enumerated in the same place or 'locally born' in 1961 census. Whereas in 1971, 70.31 per cent of rural and 63.85 per cent of urban population are 'locally born.'

The data would indicate that quite a large proportion of the total population is not mobile both in 1 61 and 1971 census. It is interesting to notice that the degree of migration is less among males than among females. Of the males in the total population, during 1961 census, 76.22 per cent are enumerated in their place of birth as against 59.00 per cent of females. During 1971 census of the males in the total population, 76.78 per cent are enumerated in their place of birth as against 60.34 per cent of females. There is generally greater migration among females. In 1961 census in the rural areas, 69.75 per cent of the population is at the place of their birth; 80.20 per cent of the rural males and 59.01 per cent of the rural females have been enumerated at their place of birth. In the urban areas, 60.97 per cent of the population, or 62.97 per cent of the urban males and 58.92 per cent of the urban females have been enumerated in their place of birth. Whereas in 1971 census in the rural areas, 70.31 per cent of the population is at the place of their birth; 80.55 per cent of the rural males and 59.76 per cent of the rural females have been enumerated at their place of birth. In the urban areas, 63.85 per cent of the population, or 65.37 per cent of the urban males and 62.18 per cent of the urban females have been enumerated in their place of birth. There is a greater proportion of migration in the urban areas. The proportion of females who remain in their places of birth in the rural and urban areas are almost equal in 1961, while the proportion of rural males who have not moved out of their place of birth is much higher than that of urban males in both the census. The greater degree of migration among females is due to the custom of the bride moving to the place where her husband lives, or in other words has been explained in terms of 'marriage' and 'associational' migration. Marriage results in a large number of female moving out of their place of birth.

TABLE 4.1 : **Percentage of population born in place of enumeration 1961—1971**

	1961			1971		
	Persons	Male	Female	Persons	Male	Female
Total	67.79	76.22	59.00	68.74	76.78	60.34
Rural	69.75	80.20	59.01	70.31	80.55	59.76
Urban	60.97	62.79	58.98	63.85	65.37	62.18

The proportion of immobility or locally born population as may be seen from Tables 4.2 and 4.3 both for 1961 and 1971 census generally accounts for a major portion of the total, rural and urban population in the state. The rural areas in general have higher proportion of immobile population than in urban areas which mainly is due to the *agro-based* occupational structure. Exceptional to this rule being Bidar district, where proportions of these locally born in urban areas (74.39 per cent) (which incidentally is the highest proportion among the districts) is slightly higher than that in rural areas (73.77 per cent). As against to that in 1961 census also Bidar district, where proportions of those locally born in urban areas (74.82 per cent) (which incidentally is the highest proportion among the districts) is slightly higher than that in rural areas (72.72 per cent). Coorg district has the lowest proportion of locally born persons in all the areas and in fact urban population has shown a higher mobility with its only 42.61 per cent of locally born persons.

The sex ratio of locally born persons (i.e., famales per 1,000 males is high in all the areas, i.e., 963,954 and 1,004 females per 1,000 males in total, rural and urban areas respectively in 1961 census, in South Kanara district. Similarly in Tumkur district is the lowest among the districts with 675, 666 and 783 in total,

TABLE 4.2 : **Migration in Karnataka (Percentages), 1961-71**

Type of Migration	1961				1971			
	Migrated				Migrated to			
	Rural		Urban		Rural		Urban	
	Male	Female	Male	Female	Male	Female	Male	Female
Non-migrant to:								
Rural	31.58	22.60	—	—	30.93	22.29	—	—
Urban	—	—	7.33	6.28	—	—	8.31	7.21
Intra-district Migrants:								
Rural	4.95	11.67	1.23	1.46	4.74	10.59	1.33	1.46
Urban	0.35	0.56	0.51	0.58	0.51	0.90	0.46	0.52
Inter-district Migrants:								
Rural	1.23	1.91	0.68	0.62	1.04	1.94	0.72	0.67
Urban	0.20	0.25	0.64	0.66	0.29	0.40	0.78	0.80
Inter-state Migrants:								
Rural	0.81	1.04	0.66	0.52	0.59	0.89	0.47	0.37
Urban	0.14	0.13	0.56	0.49	0.23	0.22	0.60	0.53

Total population: 23,586,772 (1961 census) (100%); 29,299,014 (1971 census) (100%)

Source: 1. K. Balasubramanyam, *Census of India, 1961, Vol. XI, Mysore, Part II-C* (*ii*), *Table-D-II, Migration Tables*, 1967, Delhi.

2. P. Padmanabha, Director of Census Operation, *Census of India, 1971, Mysore, Series 14, Mysore, Part II-D, Migration Tables*, 1981, Delhi.

Note: Population categorised by census as unclassifiable belonging to neither urban nor rural categories are not included in the table, but the total population figures include them also.

TABLE 4.3 : **Intra-state migration in Karnataka, 1961-1971 (Percentages)**

Type of Migration	Migrated to							
	1961 (Census)				1971 (Census)			
	Rural		Urban		Rural		Urban	
	Male	Female	Male	Female	Male	Female	Male	Female
Intra-district Migrants:								
Rural	17.99	42.37	4.48	5.30	17.42	38.94	4.88	5.38
Urban	1.28	2.05	1.85	2.09	1.87	3.29	1.71	1.89
Inter-district Migrants:								
Rural	4.46	6.92	2.48	2.25	3.83	7.15	2.65	2.46
Urban	0.72	0.90	2.32	2.40	1.08	1.45	2.86	2.96

Total population: 6,494,543 (100%) (1961 census)
7,970,868 (100%) (1971 census)

Source: 1. Table-D-II, Census of India, 1961, Vol. XI, Mysore, Part II-C (ii), Migration Tables.
2. Tables-D-I, Census of India, 1971, Series-14, Mysore, Part-II-D, Migration Tables.

Note: Population categorised by census as unclassifiable belonging to neither urban nor rural categories are not included in the table, but the total population figure includes them also.

among the districts both in 1961 and 1971 census with 666,637 and 899 in total, rural and urban areas respectively in 1961 and as against to it in 1971 census 637, 608 and 836 in total, rural and urban areas respectively. Even in 1971 census South Kanara districts stands first in sex-ratio with 953, 946, and 978 in total, rural and urban areas respectively.

The total percentage of immigrants in the state including those born outside India and those who are unclassifiable would be 4.67 per cent in 1961 and 4.05 per cent in 1971 census. It will be noticed from the data that the percentage of immigrants to the total population is particularly high in the districts of Bangalore, Bellary, Coorg, Kolar and Shimoga. The immigration into Bangalore Metropolitan area and is largely due to the industrial complex that exists in this area. The district of Bellary attracts a large element of immigrations mainly into the rural areas due to the irrigation potentialities there. The districts of Coorg and Shimoga attract immigrants due to the vast plantations that require labour in these two districts. Kolar district has a large element of immigration due to the existence of Kolar Gold Mines in that district. However, the proportion of immigrants to the total population is not considerable excepting in the districts of Bangalore and Coorg. By and large, therefore, immigration, as such, does not constitute a major determinant in the size of the population of the districts in the state.

Of the migrants within the district, 29.80 per cent are males and 70.20 per cent are females, who have migrated from one rural area to another rural area within the same district in 1961. Whereas in 1971 census 30.91 per cent are males and 69.09 per cent are females. The high proportion of females support the general conclusion made earlier that the migration is more social than economic and mainly due to marriage. The proportion of women increases with the duration. The proportions between males and females are approximately equal only in the one year and less category. This preponderance of females in all the durations is again an indication of the influence of economic factors on migration within the same district is not prominent. The seasonal migration caused by agricultural operations would not be fully reflected in the data as the enumeration in March would only catch the tail end of the 'Rabi' season. In those districts where the 'Rabi' crop is important, short duration migration is prominent. These are Belgaum, Bijapur, Dharwar and Gulbarga mainly.

Rural to urban migration within the same district due to marriage is very much less prominent in the rural to urban migration pattern. The main motivation for migration from the rural areas to the urban is economic. Bangalore district has the highest number of such migrants as is to be expected since the industrialisation in and around Bangalore city is a strong influence. The districts of Dharwar, Bijapur, South Kanara, Belgaum, and Mysore have also large number of such migrants. Table 4.2 gives the detailed distributions of migrants and non-migrant populations for both the sexes. Largest proportion of Karnataka population is constituted of non-migrant rural population. The inter-district and inter-state immigrants constitute higher proportion in rural to rural migration in both the above mentioned categories. The intra-district rural to rural female migrants are second largest. This may be due to the marital migration and patrilocal residence. This percentage rapidly falls in inter-district migration. When migrants alone are considered (Table 4.3) intra-district rural-rural migration is most frequent (C.F. Kshirasagar 1973, NSS, 1960, Zachariah 1964, Vidyasagar 1978). The difference between males and females is largest in rural-rural migration. In all other types of migrations the gap closes in and in only inter-district rural-urban migration males constitute greater percentage than females. Another important feature is that rural-rural migration is most frequent in both inter- and intra-district migration. In inter-state immigration it is least frequent.

The following statement brings out movement from rural to rural, rural to urban, urban to rural, and urban to urban areas in 1971 census.

About 62 per cent of the total male migrants move to rural areas (53 per cent from rural to rural and 9 per cent from urban to rural) whereas this percentage goes up to 77 per cent for females (70 per cent from rural to rural and 7 per cent from urban to rural). On the other hand 23 per cent (13 per cent from

TABLE 4.4 : **Inter-state migration to Karnataka, 1971**

Place of last residence	Males enumerated in			Females enumerated in		
	Rural	Urban	Total	Rural	Urban	Total
Rural	1,817,930 (52.74)	685,280 (19.88)	2,503,210 (72.62)	3,952,070 (69.56)	716,200 (12.61)	4,688,207 (82.17)
Urban	322,330 (9.35)	621,395 (19.03)	943,725 (27.38)	418,020 (7.36)	595,055 (10.47)	1,013,075 (17.85)
Total	(62.09)	(37.91)	(100.00)	(76.92)	(23.08)	(100.00)

Note: (i) The percentage to total migrants of each sex is given within brackets.

(ii) Figures of unclassifiable last place of residence are excluded.

rural to urban, 10 per cent from urban to urban) of the female migrants move to urban areas as against 38 per cent (20 per cent rural to urban, 18 per cent urban to urban) for males. Here, it is observed that the movement of males is more than that of females to urban areas where more job opportunities and educational facilities are available. Females move mainly in a connection with family and other social reasons rather than for employment. If we compare this movement within rural areas females move less from urban to rural than males (9.35 per cent males and 7.36 per cent females). The reason for this higher mobility among males may be seasonal migrations of males for contract jobs. Also male students may be moving to urban areas for education and on completion, returning home.

Table 4.5 gives the sex ratio in migrant population by types of movement during 1971 census.

TABLE 4.5 : **Number of females per thousand males, 1971**

Last residence	Place of enumeration		
	Rural	Urban	Total
Rural	2,174	1,045	1,865
Urban	1,297	958	1,073
Total	2,042	1,004	1,648

Note: Figures pertaining to unclassifiable place of last residence not included.

Marriage migration forms an important component of total migration and this is largely responsible for the imbalances in the sex ratio of migrant population. The sex ratio among migrants as may be seen from Table 4.5 is 1,648 which is highly in favour of females. The sex ratio in different types of movements, namely, rural to rural (2,174), urban to rural (1,279) and rural to urban (1,045) are also significantly higher in favour of females. In the urban to urban (958) movement alone we see that the sex ratio is in favour of males. The high sex ratio in the rural to rural movement in favour of females indicates the intensity of marriage migration of females between rural to rural areas which is not uncommon in the background that our population is predominantly rural. The different standards of life other social factors in rural and urban areas may act as a deterrent for the marriages taking place between these two areas thus resulting in relatively lesser degree movement. Further the lesser movement of males from urban to rural areas and higher mobility of males seasonal and urban to urban areas in search of better employment, for education, etc., are some of the reasons attributable for the varying sex ratios among migrants of different types.

Correlates of migration

Table 4.6 gives the inter-correlation matrix of these variables. Only male migration is considered because the female marital migration would distort the correlations. The zero order correlations with percentage of non-migrants in district as weak on variables; percentage of agricultural labourers; density per square mile; slightly high but still weak on birth rate; moderate on gross foodgrain production per acre; and considerably high on percentage of literates and persons in primary sector occupations. All except density and people in primary sector occupation are negatively correlated. That is, the more the literacy, lesser will be sedentary population in a district and people in agricultural occupations, and higher will be the intra-district rural-urban and urban-rural migrations. The more the people involved in primary sector occupations in a district the lesser will be the urban to urban migration in it. More the gross production of foodgrains in a district, lesser will be people dependent on agricultural wages, more will be the urban to rural migrants and lesser will be the sedentary population. As the urban-rural migration in a district increases the sedentary population in a district decreases. Because of the moderately high correlation (about 0.5) of this with other types of migration this can be used as a maker among the migration variables used here. When the other variables are controlled, density per square mile increases in its explanatory power (as increase in partial **R-square in** Table 4.7), and that of literacy and people in

TABLE 4.6 : **Inter-correlation matrix between migration and six other selected variables**

Variables											
1	2	3	4	5	6	7	8	9	10	11	12
—	−0.358	−0.171	−0.481	−0.211	0.171	−0.262	−0.262	0.642	−0.459	−0.111	−0.003
		0.506	0.643	−0.096	−0.213	0.470	0.739	−0.253	0.229	0.685	0.405
			0.412	0.541	0.394	0.582	0.594	−0.369	−0.112	0.393	0.227
				0.257	−0.324	0.577	0.755	−0.265	0.392	0.091	0.256
					0.454	0.444	0.256	−0.570	−0.145	−0.063	0.076
						0.217	−0.007	−0.122	−0.596	0.313	−0.338
							0.513	−0.592	0.215	0.306	−0.079
								−0.120	0.163	0.374	0.282
									−0.123	−0.279	−0.266
										−0.276	−0.266
											0.204
											–

Note: Names of the variables:

1. Percentage of non-migrants in the district.

TABLE 4.6—*Contd.*

2. Percentage of intra-district rural to rural migration in the total population.
3. Percentage of intra-district rural to urban migrants in the total population.
4. Percentage of intra-district urban to rural migrants in the total population.
5. Percentage of intra-district urban to urban migrants in the total population.
6. Density of population per square mile.
7. Percentage of literates in the total population.
8. Births per 1,000 people in 1960 and 1970.
9. Percentage of people in agricultural occupations.
10. Per capita foodgrain production per acre (in kg.).
11. Area sown twice to the total area cropped.
12. Percentage of households dependent on agricultural wages.

Sources:

1-5 Table-D-II, Census of India, 1961, Vol. XI, Mysore, Part II-C (ii), Migration Tables.
6. Statement II-32, Census of India, 1961, Vol. XI, Mysore, Part I (A), General Report.
7. Statement VII-I, Census of India, 1961, Vol. XI, Mysore, Part I (A), General Report.
8. Table-8.4, Number of live births in 1960, VIII, Public Health and Vital Statistics, Statistical Abstract of Mysore, 1960-61, Department of Statistics, Government of Mysore (1963).
9. Statement X-39, Census of India, 1961, Vol. XI, Mysore, Part I (A), General Report.
10. Statement X-64, Census of India, 1961, Vol. XI, Mysore, Part I (A), General Report.
11. Statement X-58, Census of India, 1961, Vol. XI, Mysore, Part I (A), General Report.
12. Statement X-63, Census of India, 1961, Vol. XI, Mysore, Part I (A), General Report.

TABLE 4.7 : **Partial R-squares**

	Density per square mile	Literate in the district	Births per thousand	Per cent in agricultural occupation	Per acre food-grains produ-ction	Area sown twice as a percentage to net area cropped	Population dependent in agricul-tural wages
Percentage of non-migrants in the district	0.283	0.511	0.075	0.056	0.046	0.042	0.042
Percentage of intra-disirict rural to rural migration	0·429	0.080	0.420	0.090	0.019	0.718	0.011
Percentage intra-district rural-urban migrants	0.159	0.036	0.178	0.008	0.013	0.008	0.086
Percentage of intra-district urban-rural migrants	0.310	0.157	0.478	0.013	0.026	0.096	0.000
Percentage of urban-urban migrants	0.353	0.000	0.244	0.397	0.076	0.523	0.048

agricultural occupations, decreases. The inter-correlations between migration variables are considerably high.

The rural-rural migration in a district is highly and positively correlated with urban-rural migration and births per thousand population, moderately and positively correlated with rural-urban migration, literacy, and population depending on agricultural wages. Other variables, like density per square mile (negatively) percentage in agricultural occupation (negatively), gross production per acre (positively) are weakly correlated. Partial R-squares shows that the influence of density per square mile and acres sown twice increases when other variables are controlled, and births per thousand shows a decrease (Table 4.7). Other variables lose their significance.

All the correlations are lesser in magnitude in case of rural to urban migration. Literacy and births per thousand and rural migration and moderately and positively correlated with rural-urban migration. Variation in the rural to urban migration is least accounted for by chosen variables are partialled out on others. Urban-urban migration is highly correlated with percentage in agricultural occupations (negatively) and rural urban migration (positively). Among other variables correlated with it, density and percentage of literates are worth mentioning and both area positively correlated. The area sown twice as a percentage of net area cropped show considerable explanatory power when other variables are controlled. But when the same is partialled out on other migration variables it loses its significance. Density per square mile and per cent in agricultural occupation shows an increase.

Overall density per square mile, literacy, births per thousand are important variables in understanding the variance in all types of migration. The chosen variables account for 86 per cent of variation in the sedentary population in a district. The explanatory capacity of these variables is at its maximum (90 per cent, Table 4.8) in rural to rural migration and at its minimum (61 per cent, Table 4.8) in case of rural to urban migration. Since most of the variables used in analysis are agrarian in nature, this is to be expected.

The correlation analysis of different types of intra-district migrations and other variables shows that the proportion of non-migrants in a district are moderately and negatively correlated with literates in a district and primary sector occupations. About 90 per cent of variance in rural to rural migration in a district is accounted for by the chosen variables. Density per square mile, literacy, births per thousand population are important variables in understanding all types of migration. The rural to urban migration is least explained by the variables considered since the variables used in the analysis are agrarian in nature. Urban to rural migration, because of its high correlations with all other types of migration in a district, could be used as a maker.

TABLE 4.8 : **R-squares and R-bar-squares of different migration types in a district**

	R-Square	R-bar-square
1 Sedentary population in a district	0.86	0.76
2 Rural to rural migration in a district	0.90	0.84
3 Rural to urban migration in a district	0.61	0.36
4 Urban to rural migration in a district	0.80	0.67
5 Urban to urban migration in a district	0.77	0.62

Note: Six variables are used in the calculations namely (in a district): (1) Density; (2) Literacy; (3) Births per thousand population; (4) Percentage in agricultural occupations; (5) Gross production and foodgrains per acre; (6) Percentage of people dependent on agricultural wages.

TABLE 4.9 : **Proportion of "locally born" persons and its sex ratio in state and districts—1961**

	Proportion of locally born			Sex ratio of locally born (F/M × 1000)		
	Total	Rural	Urban	Total	Rural	Urban
1	2	3	4	5	6	7
Bangalore	62.50	73.24	58.40	772	687	873
Belgaum	68.79	69.89	63.75	687	664	812
Bellary	70.59	73.54	60.47	794	776	874
Bidar	72.98	72.72	74.82	666	637	899
Bijapur	65.87	66.51	62.18	719	702	801
Chickmagalur	58.81	69.29	56.11	757	744	841
Chitradurga	70.53	73.53	56.30	741	721	839
Coorg	50.95	52.22	42.61	790	776	911
Dharwar	64.90	66.09	61.82	743	712	838
Gulbarga	70.15	70.88	66.34	691	663	861
Hassan	68.82	70.58	55.93	705	695	798
Kolar	71.30	72.85	66.00	709	676	846
Mandya	71.02	72.81	56.74	695	687	788
Mysore	74.33	75.09	69.00	752	724	849

TABLE 4.9—(*Contd.*)

1	2	3	4	5	6	7
North Kanara	59.44	60.07	56.45	788	763	928
Raichur	71.61	71.91	69.29	741	729	861
Shimoga	57.70	63.35	41.30	767	745	874
South Kanara	67.53	67.56	67.43	963	954	1004
Tumkur	71.31	72.53	60.47	675	666	783
STATE	67.79	69.75	60.97	742	716	857

TABLE 4.10 : **Proportion of "locally born" persons and its sex ratio by R/U in state and districts—1971**

	Proportion of locally born persons			Sex ratio of locally born persons		
	Total	Rural	Urban	Total	Rural	Urban
1	2	3	4	5	6	7
Bangalore	66.92	71.02	63.63	813	718	909
Belgaum	67.39	68.76	62.11	685	664	780
Bellary	71.27	71.97	69.43	781	750	874
Bidar	73.53	73.37	74.39	637	608	836
Bijapur	66.95	67.86	56.96	733	714	809
Chickmagalur	62.91	63.76	58.27	775	767	827
Chitradurga	70.29	73.16	58.96	764	738	869
Coorg	56.14	57.64	47.94	816	804	899
Dharwar	64.81	65.75	62.75	756	722	839
Gulbarga	72.96	73.57	70.13	695	667	842
Hassan	70.61	72.52	58.58	702	687	826
Kolar	73.19	74.47	68.29	694	661	850
Mandya	72.55	74.82	58.33	712	702	805
Mysore	72.92	77.01	68.79	752	716	881

TABLE 4.10—(*Contd.*)

1	2	3	4	5	6	7
North Kanara	61.23	62.40	55.80	797	775	927
Raichur	70.79	70.82	70.68	767	750	866
Shimoga	60.45	62.44	54.02	779	752	886
South Kanara	68.82	68.95	68.31	953	946	978
Tumkur	70.56	72.19	58.23	695	681	841
TATE	68.74	70.31	63.85	752	721	877

5

INTERNAL MIGRATION AND POPULATION REDISTRIBUTION IN INDIA

THIS SECTION examines the impact on the redistribution of population on the basis of internal migration based on the data of preceding 1971 census. This redistribution does not explain in true sense the quantum and characteristics at various points of time which usually help determining the real redistribution.[1] However, it defines the directions and quantum in some significance as how the population has been displaced in the country. The main emphasis is the identification of characteristics mostly on the consideration of inter-district and intra-district displacements. Besides, a view is presented with the population shift to urban centres and agglomerations of population 100,000 and above leading to inter-state migration.

Migration composition and urban growth

Most people are familiar with the important function of the level of migration as a determinant of urban-regional growth. The composition of migration streams is also interrelated with rural-urban and inter-urban growth differentials. We encounter this last idea in discussions of regional disparities, where we often read statements to the effect that migration contributes to a spiral of decline among some regions by drawing off the more productive segments of their populations.

We should locate the role of migration within the context of a broader growth model; since it is only one of several relevant factors and is itself a response to growth differentials.

Chart-I presents a highly simplified scheme of interrelations among selected determinants of population growth differentials among regions. This chart shows the composition of migration as being but one of a network of interrelated growth determinants. In terms of the amount of growth variance it explains, it may be significantly less important than several of the factors mentioned in the chart; but we believe it to be a necessary condition of the maintenance of regional economic structural differences, and in regional labour adjustments to economic structural changes (in an open system of regions). Though the interaction of the composition of migration with economic structure, the former influences (and is influenced by) economic growth differences. There is also a more indirect path of influence of migration composition of economic growth differences through the impact of the former on population growth differences.

Rural urban characteristics

In rural and urban areas of the country, the movements are typically various due to differences in opportunities. In rural areas immigrants to total rural population is high mostly in the majority of districts of Punjab, Haryana, Assam (16.01—24.00 per cent), parts of North Bengal (10—24 per cent), Maharashtra, Madhya Pradesh (10.01—16 per cent) and Tripura. On contrary, low ratio of rural migrants are noticed mainly in the thickly populated zones of Bihar, Andhra Pradesh, Tamil Nadu and Rajasthan in large number of districts in particular to name a few states. The variations in life-time inter-state net migration rates in rural and urban areas can be seen from Tables 5.1 and 5.2.

Proportions in urban areas are quite different. Maharashtra being industrially in favourable position shows very high proportion of urban migrants (81.98 per cent) to total in-migrants. Delhi and Chandigarh, being highly urbanised are responsible for more than 90 per cent of such populations. West Bengal counting greatly on its Calcutta. Howrah complex and the industrial belt hardly account for 52.05 per cent of urban migrants. Gujarat (73.81 per cent) and Tamil Nadu (66.89 per cent) comparatively show different situations.

CHART—I

Selected determinants of growth differentials among a set of regions

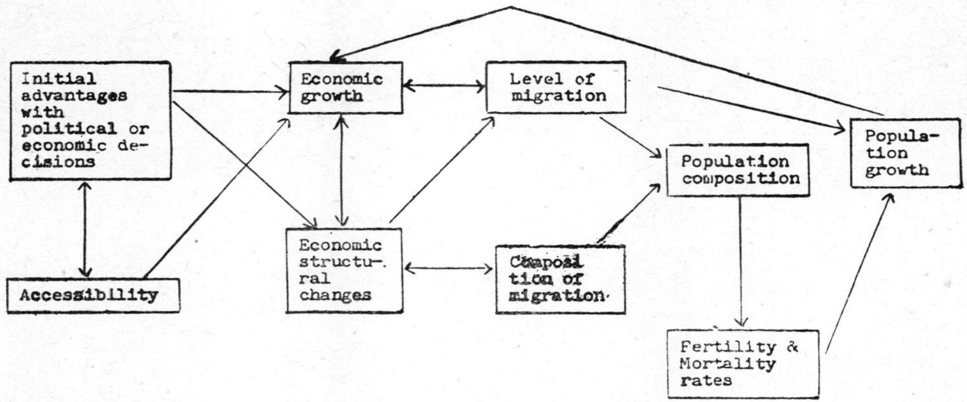

Note: Inside each box is the name given to a constellation of determinants. Arrows show the hypothesized major directions of influence between particular sets of determinants. Two headed arrows indicate major influence flowing in both directions. A given set of determinants is only partly influenced by another, and the former normally has substantial variation that is independent of other factors mentioned in the chart. Fertility and mortality rates would be a prime example of such "autonomous" variations.

Inter-district and intra-district patterns

A very important reflection of migrants is ruled out from the analysis of two variables, viz., intra-district (short distance) and inter-district (long distance) migration in the political frame of districts. If these two types are assessed further by supplementary rigorous field study data, probably more insight into the migration type in India can be established. Obviously, the mapping of these two variables indicate certain typical sociological significance of the redistribution of people in this context.

TABLE 5.1 : **Life-time inter-state net migration rates by sex and by rural/urban in 1961 and 1971 census**

State/Union Territories/India	Rural			
	Males		Females	
	1961	1971	1961	1971
Andhra Pradesh	−12.9	−11.1	−8.2	−7.7
Assam and Meghalaya	34.5	27.0	17.5	13.9
Bihar	−45.3	−32.3	−15.4	−12.3
Gujarat	−17.3	−13.5	−11.5	−11.8
Jammu and Kashmir	−14.6	4.1	−4.7	1.7
Kerala	−21.8	−24.2	−5.5	−9.4
Madhya Pradesh	6.4	5.2	4.8	3.4
Maharashtra	−1.9	−0.5	−2.3	−1.9
Mysore	2.5	−1.7	0.4	−0.8
Orissa	−19.0	−3.7	−6.0	3.2
Punjab Group	−37.2	−31.8	−21.4	−16.6
Rajasthan	−27.7	−25.8	−20.6	−16.2
Tamil Nadu	−23.5	−15.2	−19.2	−9.9
Uttar Pradesh	−30.0	−30.7	−9.4	−11.5
West Bengal	18.2	9.0	4.1	2.2
Delhi	75.9	198.5	56.9	104.2
Nagaland and Union Territories	26.9	33.5	21.6	14.2
ALL INDIA	−15.9	−13.2	−7.3	−6.0

Note: Figures with minus sign indicates net out-migration rate.

Source: G.K. Mehrotra, Office of the Registrar General, India, Census of India, 1971, Series 1, India, Special Monograph No. 1, Birth Place Migration in India, 1974, Delhi.

TABLE 5.2 : Life-time inter-state net migration rates by sex and by rural/urban in 1961 and 1971 census

States/India	Urban			
	Males		Females	
	1961	1971	1961	1971
Andhra Pradesh	4.7	0.5	4.8	5.5
Assam and Meghalaya	134.6	125.5	28.5	28.0
Bihar	15.9	6.1	37.2	19.4
Gujarat	11.8	33.9	−5.7	11.5
Jammu and Kashmir	−33.3	−16.0	−22.8	19.0
Kerala	−98.9	−118.2	−53.8	−77.8
Madhya Pradesh	124.6	107.2	88.7	83.7
Maharashtra	185.9	164.2	119.8	107.9
Mysore	47.7	20.2	35.9	10.5
Orissa	57.2	70.7	62.9	83.5
Punjab Group	−7.8	19.3	−31.4	−4.8
Rajasthan	−23.5	−19.1	−19.0	−15.8
Tamil Nadu	4.1	10.1	0.8	4.6
Uttar Pradesh	−27.1	−45.4	−8.7	−27.2
West Bengal	208.5	125.6	80.6	34.7
Delhi	360.2	336.1	281.5	259.1
Nagaland and Union Territory	16.8	67.3	−22.5	−51.5
ALL INDIA	70.0	54.9	37.5	29.1

Note: Figures with minus sign indicates net out-migration rate.

Source: G.K. Mehrotra, Office of the Registrar General, India, Census of India, 1971, Series 1, India, Special Monograph No. 1, Birth Place Migration in India, 1974, Delhi.

Intra-district pattern

The evaluation of 357 districts of 1971 Census on intra-district movement indicates high proportion of females in rural and males in urban. Largely the contention is shifting females to husbands' house while in case of males various other accords may be established on this consideration. Probably, shifting of females after marriage from rural parents' house to rural husbands' house is more appropriate. On the contrary, intensity of female migration from rural house to urban is comparatively weak. This needs more probing.

More important for any meaningful consideration is the movement of males in the intra-district migration. The predominance of female migration in rural areas to short distance movement besides marriage phenomena, a large proportion may belong to female agricultural labour. However, it is very clear that this type assists to be a greater extent in establishing class and seeks boundaries in the country on the basis of migration.

Inter-district pattern

The movement of migrants from one district to another district of the same state/U.T. indicates a response to the variation in the economic development of the regions. If 25.01 per cent and above is the limit of high movements in inter-district movement 20° parallel and 80° meridian from an enclave over India which retains high percentage of migrants resided in other districts o the state of enumeration to total migrants. This area falls mostly over Uttar Pradesh, Haryana, Punjab, Himachal Pradesh, Rajasthan, Gujarat, Madhya Pradesh and Maharashtra. On the contrary, the entire eastern region comprising Bihar, West Bengal, Orissa, and North Eastern hill region below 20 per cent is conspicuous. However, certain sporadic districts claim above 25 per cent share in other areas in South India.

In this type of movement, it is estimated that in the rural and urban sectors proportions of female migrants to total female migrants is higher. Similar trend is established in male migrants also. Probably in this type of movement family displacement may be ruled out.

Urban centres and agglomerations

The population of migrants in urban centres and agglomerations (100,000 and above) in the country is an indication of disparity between development and employment. If data is synthesised, the following characteristics are noted.

Extra-territorial and territorial

(i) The feature more relevant is the distribution related to the partition of the country and its impact on socio-demographic relation of the past.[2] The urban migrants if assessed according to place of birth, the migrants having place of birth outside India distributed mostly in the towns of north and western India.[3] In this frame, maximum concentration of migrants is observed in the towns of Calcutta agglomerations, Delhi, Agartala, towns of Punjab, Haryana, Rajasthan and Uttar Pradesh. Secondary concentrations are over Gujarat, Maharashtra and Madhya Pradesh. A feeble concentration is also over Kerala and Tamil Nadu towns.

(ii) The other population category belonging to the territorial limits of India, i.e., whose last residence in other states but enumerated in particular state (beyond the state of enumeration) is maximum (54.50) in Greater Bombay, Calcutta UA (44.45 per cent), Delhi UA (74.78 per cent) and Chandigarh (96.98 per cent) to cite a few centres.

Economic status significance

The economic status attributes in this consideration is the working and non-working level with educational attainment of the migrants. The description is gloomy to a greater extent. If all the towns for which data are considered on functional basis, certain important issues emerge of the redistribution in urban agglomerations in the categories of poly-functional, bi-functional and uni-functional centres.[4]

The poly-functional towns provide a comparatively diversified infrastructure to migrants for sustenance. Such infrastructures are very weak at such centres which have failed to display working and non-working proportions of migrants in the country. Since, these centres are mostly located in the agricultural tracts whose articulation of development is not dynamic[5] leave the migrants to under-development and unnourished. In this category, the non-working migrants represent higher proportions over working. Even, the port towns show this incidence to a greater degree.

Among the bifunctional towns, the structure of articulations is limited to either service, industry or commerce. In this sector also, although the proportion of non-working migrants is comparatively higher than the working, the absorption of migrants according to educational levels in the working sector is low. At such centres the proportions of migrants having non-working status is very high.

Thirdly, the uni-functional centres in the country which are represented solely by either industrial or service in majority such as Calcutta, Bombay or steel towns or a few mining towns provide a major base to migrants.

In this process of redistribution in urban areas, it may be remarked that the urban working migrants to total urban migrants lies mostly in the range of 35-60 per cent in the country except Rajasthan and Uttar Pradesh where it is below 35 per cent. In this social set-up, migrants having primary and middle level education have large base of employment, followed by illiterates, matriculations, higher secondary, diploma, graduate and post-graduate and other technical degree personnel. The literates without educational level have their conspicuous share.

National perspective

A look on the 1961 and 1971 birth place statistics at the national level indicates variations in female movement. Variation in urban sector stood at 21.47 per cent in total in which female migration accounted for an increase of 25.25 per cent as represented by Table 5.3. It is recognised that the rural sector being even, the urban was little modulated in the male and female sectors. If, in fact, undesirable effects of urban development have been experienced it may be worthwhile to revaluate the nature of this development in male and female variations.

Again across the borders of states in terms of gain and loss, the country illustrates five defined divisions of areas (Table 5.2). Here the total disparity in development is reflected in its manifold character both political and socio-economic. In strict sense, the developed states such as Maharashtra which was received about 52.16 per cent net migrants being industrially rich (at least high in number of factories) indicates a progressive response to development attracting migrants. Others such as Punjab and

Haryana being agriculturally developed (to some extent industrially) show less inward capability. Other areas such as Assam, Tripura, Delhi and Chandigarh are the reflections of arrivals in high proportions on many socio-economic accords.

TABLE 5.3 : **India**

Migrants (1961-71)	1961 and 1971 (Millions)			Per cent Variations		
	Total	Male	Female	Total	Male	Female
Total	144.8 (166.7)	46.9 (53.7)	97.9 (113.0)	15.66	15.24	15.87
Rural	109.4 (123.9)	28.2 (31.7)	81.2 (92.2)	13.78	13.32	13.95
Urban	35.4 (42.8)	18.7 (22.0)	16.7 (20.8)	21.47	18.12	25.25

Source: D-II Table (Place of birth) 1961
D-I Table (Place of birth) 1971.

Migration flow types and reflections

In this connection, the evaluation of a matrix on the basis of place of birth in the inter-state terms in four streams viz., (i) rural to rural, (ii) rural-urban, (iii) urban-urban, and (iv) urban-rural, if considered a considerable insight can be had in the developments.

(i) *Rural to Rural*: Flow especially of females is high from Karnataka to Andhra Pradesh (95 thousand) followed by Maharashtra to Andhra Pradesh (37 thousand), Tamil Nadu to Andhra Pradesh (34 thousand), from Uttar Pradesh to Madhya Pradesh (180 thousand), Punjab to Haryana (87 thousand), Delhi to Haryana (33 thousand) and Uttar Pradesh to Haryana (91 thousand).

Flow of males from Bihar to Assam (112 thousand) is very high. Contribution of Uttar Pradesh and West Bengal to Assam in this is 24 and 20 thousand respectively. Uttar Pradesh contributes males in Madhya Pradesh to the tune of 83 thousand which is sociologically important.

TABLE 5.4 : **Percentage net migration to gross migration**

Receiving Areas	Percentage Range	Losing Areas
Assam (77.51), Tripura (90.08) Andaman and Nicobar Island (91.99), Arunachal Pradesh (93.69), Chandigarh (80.88)	75.01 and above	
Maharashtra (52.16), Manipur (52.88), Meghalaya (59.49), Nagaland (74.96), West Bengal (74.96), Delhi (74.99), Lakshadweep (57.93)	50.01-75.00	Kerala (55.39)
Haryana (25.37), Madhya Pradesh, (36.62), Sikkim (44.39), Dadar and Nagar Haveli (40.26)	25.01-50.00	Bihar (30.34), Uttar Pradesh (32.87)
Gujarat (4.37), Jammu and Kashmir (16.06), Karnataka (2.91), Orissa (8.63), Punjab (16.55), Pondicherry (9.37)	25.00 and below	Andhra Pradesh (17.43), Himachal Pradesh (10.16), Rajasthan (9.97), Tamil Nadu (5.56), Goa, Daman and Diu (5.14)

Source: Net Migration based on Table-D-1 (place of birth) of 1971 census.

1. A Mitra, Registrar General and Ex-Officio Census Commissioner for India, Census of India, 1961, Vol. I, India, Part II-C (ii), Migration Tables, D-II-Tables, India, 1966.
2. A Chandra Sekhar, Registrar General and Census Commissioner, Census of India, 1971, Series I-India, Part II-D (i), Migration Tables (Tables-D-I to D-IV); (D-II Tables, India, 1979).

(ii) *Rural to Urban*: Flow distribution among male is pronounced in general. In some characteristic cases Tamil

Nadu to Andhra Pradesh (17,000 males), Karnataka to Andhra Pradesh (14,000), Kerala to Andhra Pradesh (11,000), Bihar to Assam (51,000), is the move followed by Uttar Pradesh to Assam (17,000), Bihar (55,000), highest being to Madhya Pradesh (110,000) and Maharashtra (333,000) males.

Female contribution in this direction is high from Gujarat to Maharashtra (147,000), Karnataka to Maharashtra (110,000), as examples.

(iii) *Urban to Urban*: Distribution is generally even both in males and females with narrow margins. Important trends lie between Gujarat to Maharashtra (128,000 males: 118,000 females) towards high balance. This is maintained in terms of Uttar Pradesh to Maharashtra, Karnataka to Maharashtra and Tamil Nadu to Maharashtra and Madhya Pradesh to Maharashtra. In some cases female migrants out-number males.

(iv) *Urban to Rural*: Urban to rural direction is generally weak. Significant contributors (above 10 thousand males and females) are Maharashtra to Gujarat, Tamil Nadu to Andhra Pradesh, Maharashtra to Madhya Pradesh, Uttar Pradesh to Madhya Pradesh, Maharashtra to Karnataka, Tamil Nadu to Karnataka and *vice-versa* and Kerala to Tamil Nadu are notable.

These trends show that the displacement to a greater degree in the above sectoral systems are geographically responsive. However, certain exceptions do occur.

Natural increase and migration

The migration system in the country is low which signifies some relation of economic development disparity and shift in population. The quantum of migration both inward and outward of 0-9 years duration is assessed in a particular state, an important indication is achieved to support the above view. The rise in population is due to natural increase where migration does not play a strong input (Table 5.5).

The depressed states in view of total development which are mostly losing in terms of inter-state migration show aptly inter-state position of out-migration high in absolute terms in Uttar Pradesh, Bihar, Kerala and Rajasthan where the components of natural increase is uniformly high. Taking into consideration the prosperous states of Punjab and Haryana, it is interesting to

TABLE 5.5 : **Percentage share of migration and natural increase to total variation, 1961—71**

Gaining States										Losing States				
States/U.T.	Percentage of share				States/U.T.	Percentage of share				States/U.T.	Percentage of share			
	In	Out	Net	NI		In	Out	Net	NI		In	Out	Net	NI
Assam	7	4	3	97	West Bengal	9	6	3	97	Andhra Pradesh	5	7	−2	102
Gujarat	7	6	1	99	Andaman & Nicobar Islands	45	7	38	62	Bihar	5	10	−5	105
Haryana	20	17	3	97	Arunachal Pradesh	22	4	18	82	Himachal Pradesh	16	19	−3	103
Madhya Pradesh	9	6	3	97	Chandigarh	94	22	72	28	Jammu and Kashmir	5	6	−1	101
Maharashtra	13	6	7	93	Dadar & Nagar Haveli	40	11	29	71	Kerala	4	11	−7	107
Manipur	4	3	1	99	Delhi	58	17	41	59	Punjab	15	25	−10	110
Meghalaya	16	10	6	94	Lakshadweep	22	5	17	83	Rajasthan	8	11	−3	103
Mysore	10	9	1	99	Pondicherry	47	34	13	87	Tamil Nadu	6	7	−1	101
Nagaland	19	8	11	89	Goa, Daman & Diu	34	15	19	81	Tripura	5	5	–	100
Orissa	6	5	1	99						Uttar Pradesh	5	12	−7	107
Sikkim	15	11	4	96										

Source: Table-D-II, Migrants classified by place of last residence and duration of residence, 1971 census.

In : In-migrants.

Out : Out-migrants.

Net : Net Migrants-in-out.

NI : Natural Increase—Decadal variation—net migration (0-9 duration).

find high out-migration and comparatively low inward flow in Punjab while Haryana is accounting for higher inward movement than outward. On the other hand, some industrially important states like Maharashtra, West Bengal, Gujarat, Delhi and Chandigarh show more arrivals indicating strong pull due to development at various locations and infrastructure.

In this brief analysis, it is indicated that the study of redistribution in this context although presents some trends but does not direct towards the significance of migration/potentialities and economic development in the country. It is difficult to even quantify the share of migration due to economic reason.

The reflection which is obtained by the working, non-working and educational levels of migrants at urban centres to some extent indicate gaps between development and opportunities.

The parameters of study of internal movement need an overall consideration of developmental processes and communities and the level of responses and hence the data collection may demand micro synthesis. In this connection, it may be desirable to find out some way to assess the migration in households as this level is disintegrating both in rural and urban at the level of family system, religious and seeks; on the other hand, the agricultural and industrial relationships are difficult to articulate regional balance. It is essential to generate a system to study these with data so that at micro level redistribution can be established in long and short distances, within or through the points of geographic locations suitably divided in tiers to end from with economic inputs across the borders.

REFERENCES

1. (i) Census of India, Geographic Distribution of Internal Migration in India, New Delhi, 1980 (Directions B.K. Roy and Gen. Directions P. Padmanabha).

(ii) B.K. Roy, "Internal Migration in India's Manpower Resources", Net Geog. J. India, Vol. 25 (1), 1978.

(iii) B.K. Roy, "Internal Migration in India—An Evaluation of 1971 Census Data", Trans. Inst. Ind. Geog., Vol. 2 (1), 1980.

2. ILO, International Migration, 1945-1957, Geneva, 1959 pp. 108-117.

3. Census of India, 'Geographic Distribution of Internal Migration in India', op. cit., pp. 9-10 and Map No. 9.
4. Consult for such identifications in the census of India census Atlas (National Volume), 1971, Plate 40.
5. B.K. Roy, 'Potentiality of Environs of Growth Centres in India', in Balanced Regional Development, Oxford and IBH, Calcutta, 1972, pp. 66-71.

APPENDICES

Statement showing distribution of migrants (figures in '00) by different age-groups for each state/union territory by duration of residence 0-9 years—1971 census

Sex : Male

Age Group	Andhra Pradesh			Assam			Bihar			Gujarat			Haryana		
	I	O	I-O	I	O	I-O	I	O	I-O	I	O	I-O	I	O	I-O
0–2	81	83	−2	21	14	+ 7	47	59	−12	85	72	+13	73	59	+14
3–7	217	242	−25	96	67	+29	183	300	−117	200	182	+18	208	231	−23
8–12	186	249	−63	162	78	+84	198	483	−285	210	151	+59	231	225	+6
13–17	130	184	−54	120	54	+66	117	383	−266	141	147	— 6	208	171	+37
18–22	244	328	−84	246	102	+144	199	887	−688	347	272	+75	311	269	+42
23–27	255	356	−101	269	124	+145	224	827	−603	321	209	+112	282	215	+67
28–32	240	294	−54	250	127	+123	250	791	−541	292	158	+134	264	184	+80
33–37	140	221	−81	141	68	+73	181	446	−269	163	101	+62	138	128	+10
38–42	136	161	−25	111	49	+62	126	353	−227	118	87	+31	112	100	+12
43–47	77	96	−19	59	36	+23	70	156	−86	71	52	+19	52	51	+1
48–52	77	69	+8	58	32	+26	50	130	−80	61	44	+17	60	64	−4
53–57	47	27	+20	19	14	+5	37	49	−12	32	25	+7	31	31	—21

Age	Andhra Pradsh			Assam			Bihar			Gujarat			Haryana		
Group	I	O	I-O	I	O	I-O	I	O	I-O	I	O	I-O	I	O	I-O
58—62	29	39	−10	15	15	–	24	48	−24	26	34	−8	44	23	+21
63—67	11	20	−9	3	7	—4	8	18	−10	11	9	+2	18	12	+6
68—72	7	16	−9	8	4	+4	12	13	−1	14	9	+5	15	16	−1
73+	12	6	+6	8	5	+3	13	15	−2	8	7	+1	16	17	−1
Total	1889	2391	−502	1586	796	790	1739	4958	−3219	2100	1559	541	2063	1796	267

Note: (i) Figures are estimated on 1 per cent sample basis.
(ii) O denotes Out-migrants.
(iii) I denotes In-migrants.
(iv) I-O denotes Net migrants.

Statement showing distribution of migrants (figures in '00) by different age-groups for each state/union territory by duration of residence 0-9 years—1971 census

Sex : Male

Age	Himachal Pradesh			Jammu and Kashmir			Kerala			Madhya Pradesh			Maharashtra		
Group	I	O	I-O	I	O	I-O	I	O	I-O	I	O	I-O	I	O	I-O
0–2	24	21	+3	32	12	+20	14	74	–60	80	73	+7	244	156	+88
3–7	63	63	—	25	25	–	86	153	–67	335	240	+95	676	409	+267
8—12	68	52	–16	26	16	+10	100	141	—41	422	228	+194	709	394	+315
13–17	50	65	–15	24	24	–	73	164	–91	268	134	+134	615	217	+398
18–22	71	147	–76	57	49	+8	131	492	–361	514	220	+294	1601	401	+1200
23–27	94	95	–1	72	87	—15	129	560	–431	488	240	+248	1442	381	+1061
28–32	79	111	–32	63	95	–32	139	387	–248	528	274	+254	1076	381	+695
33–37	52	61	–9	26	46	–20	85	171	–86	308	145	+163	534	268	+266
38–42	46	37	+9	21	26	–5	64	120	–56	194	136	+58	383	199	+184
43–47	24	21	+3	7	15	–8	56	89	–33	113	79	+34	207	130	+77
48–52	21	14	+7	7	15	–8	34	52	–18	114	72	+42	177	128	+49
53–57	18	8	+10	1	1	–	18	22	–4	33	27	+6	76	55	+21

Age Group	Himachal Pradesh			Jammu and Kashmir			Kerala			Madhya Pradesh			Maharashtra		
	I	O	I-O	I	O	I-O	I	O	I-O	I	O	I-O	I	O	I-O
58–62	6	8	--12	2	3	–1	14	28	—14	45	26	+19	61	63	—2
63–67	2	5	.—3	–	1	–1	12	12	–	28	9	+19	22	38	–16
68–72	2	1	+1	2	2	–	3	6	–3	19	7	+12	20	22	–2
73+	3	3	–	1	4	–3	2	7	–5	14	12	+2	24	12	+12
Total	623	712	—89	366	421	–55	960	2478	–1518	3503	1922	+1581	7867	3254	4613

Notes: (i) Figures are estimated on 1 per cent sample basis.
(ii) I denotes In-migrants.
(iii) O denotes Out-migrants.
(iv) I-O denotes Net migrants

Statement showing distribution of migrants (figures in '00) by different age-groups for each state/union territory by duration of residence 0-9 years—1971 census

Sex: Male

Age	Manipur			Meghalaya			Mysore			Nagaland			Orissa		
Group	I	O	I-O	I	O	I-O	I	O	I-O	I	O	I-O	I	O	I-O
0—2	1	—	+1	3	2	+1	87	98	—11	1	3	—2	47	14	+33
3—7	2	2	—	20	7	+13	263	271	—8	6	1	+5	154	80	+74
8—12	8	4	+4	18	12	+6	271	255	+16	3	4	—1	170	100	+70
3—17	2	4	—2	13	8	+5	221	167	+54	9	1	+8	98	75	+23
18—22	12	15	—3	38	11	+27	407	382	+25	61	8	+53	179	154	+25
23—27	17	15	+2	32	28	+4	370	301	+69	64	17	+47	193	144	+49
28—32	16	6	+10	24	17	+7	329	269	+60	41	14	+27	230	158	+72
33—37	5	2	+3	14	7	+7	199	154	+45	19	6	+13	151	85	+66
38—42	4	3	+1	12	10	+2	161	142	+19	14	4	+10	122	69	+53
43—47	—	2	—2	6	7	—1	96	71	+25	9	2	+7	64	34	+30
48—52	1	2	—1	3	4	—1	79	68	+11	4	3	+1	51	35	+16
53—57	2	1	+1	1	2	—1	41	32	+9	—	1	—1	38	17	+21

Age Group	Manipur			Meghalaya			Mysore			Nagaland			Orissa		
	I	O	I-O	I	O	I-O	I	O	I-O	I	O	I-O	I	O	I-O
58—62	1	1	—	—	1	—1	55	37	+18	—	—	—	33	5	+28
63—67	1	—	+1	—	—	—	27	11	+16	—	—	—	5	3	+2
68—72	—	—	—	1	1	—	19	11	+8	—	1	—1	6	1	+5
73+	1	—	+1	2	2	—	7	7	—	—	1	—1	5	3	+2
Total	73	57	+16	187	119	+68	2032	2276	+356	231	66	+166	1546	977	+569

Note: (i) Figures are estimated on 1 per cent sample basis.
(ii) I denotes In-migrants.
(iii) O denotes Out-migrants.
(iv) I-O denotes Net-migrants.

Statement showing distribution of migrants (figures in '00) by different age-groups for each state/union territory by duration of residence 0-9 years—1971 census

Sex : Male

Age	Punjab			Rajasthan			Tamil Nadu			Tripura			Uttar Pradesh		
Group	I	O	I-O	I	O	I-O	I	O	I-O	I	O	I-O	I	O	I-O
0—2	105	86	+19	41	120	— 79	91	60	+31	2	2	—	60	211	—151
3—7	285	276	+ 9	157	293	—136	227	253	—26	11	9	+2	213	609	—396
8—12	251	322	—71	154	311	—157	185	239	—54	9	15	—6	278	799	—521
13—17	182	262	—80	124	283	—159	147	188	—41	3	9	—6	177	753	—576
18—22	320	396	—76	185	516	—331	266	373	—107	15	16	—1	346	1834	—1488
23—27	257	390	—133	149	407	—258	285	396	—111	16	17	—1	303	1737	—1434
28—32	224	348	—124	146	340	—194	237	385	—148	19	14	+5	299	1504	—1205
33—37	135	224	—89	97	182	—85	152	214	—62	6	6	—	167	719	—552
38—42	108	173	—65	64	163	—99	125	194	—69	5	6	—1	155	504	—349
43—47	58	101	—43	49	74	—25	82	111	—29	10	6	+4	74	264	—190
48—52	50	97	—47	44	84	—40	73	99	—26	3	2	+1	69	211	—142
53—57	22	49	—27	17	27	—10	24	52	—28	3	8	—5	35	96	—61

Age	Punjab			Rajasthan			Tamil Nadu			Tripura			Uttar Pradesh		
Group	I	O	I-O	I	O	I-O	I	O	I-O	I	O	I-O	I	O	I-O
58—62	24	55	—31	24	39	—15	34	40	—6	4	1	+3	42	90	—48
63—67	6	23	—17	13	10	+3	17	24	—7	1	3	—2	23	34	—11
68—72	13	16	—3	8	12	—4	12	16	—4	2	3	—1	13	36	—23
72+	9	24	—15	12	15	—3	4	9	—5	—	1	—1	26	31	—5
Total	2049	2842	—793	1284	2876	—1592	1961	2653	—692	109	118	—9	2280	9432	—7152

Note: (i) Figures are estimated on 1 per cent sample basis.
(ii) I denotes In-migrants.
(iii) O denotes Out-migrants.
(iv) I-O denotes Net-migrants.

Statement showing distribution of migrants (figures in '00) by different age groups for each state/union territory by duration of residence 0-9 years—1971 census

Sex : Male

Age	West Bengal			Andaman & Nicobar Islands			Arunachal Pradesh			Chandigarh			Dadara & Nagar Haveli		
Group	I	O	I-O	I	O	I-O	I	O	I-O	I	O	I-O	I	O	I-O
0—2	57	60	—3	—	2	—2	3	—	+3	19	6	+13	1	—	+1
3—7	246	224	+22	9	3	+6	8	2	+6	74	28	+46	3	5	—2
8—12	380	240	+140	10	40	—30	4	2	+2	71	15	+56	1	1	—
13—17	368	185	+183	7	2	+5	3	3	—	61	17	+44	2	—	+2
18—22	734	280	+454	29	1	+28	21	3	+18	127	21	+106	3	2	+1
23—27	786	325	+461	51	2	+49	25	5	+20	135	13	+122	4	—	+4
28—32	799	333	+466	31	2	+29	21	7	+14	91	25	+66	2	1	+1
33—37	432	225	+207	15	4	+11	9	5	+ 4	58	8	+50	2	—	+2
38—42	341	163	+178	10	2	+8	9	6	+ 3	39	10	+29	2	—	+2
43—47	157	105	+52	2	2	—	5	1	+4	21	3	+18	—	1	—1
48—52	140	96	+44	6	2	+4	5	—	+5	18	2	+16	2	—	+2

Age	West Bengal			Andaman & Nicobar Islands			Arunachal Pradesh			Chandigarh			Cadara & Nagar Haveli		
Gaoup	I	O	I-O	I	O	I-O	I	O	I-O	I	O	I-O	I	O	I.O
53—57	46	58	—12	4	3	+1	I	—	+1	15	2	+13	—	1	—1
58—62	47	31	+16	1	—	+1	2	—	+1	7	4	+3	—	1	—1
63—67	18	15	+3	—	—	—	—	—	—	3	—	+3	1	—	+1
68—72	10	12	—2	—	1	— 1	—	—	—	4	1	+3	—	—	—
73+	14	20	—6	—	—	—	—	—	—	3	3	—	—	—	—
Total	4575	2372	+2203	175	66	109	116	34	82	746	158	588	23	12	11

Note: (i) Figures are estimated on 1 per cent sample basis.
(ii) I denotes In-migrants.
(iii) O denotes Out-migrants.
(iv) I-O denotes Net-migrants.

Statement showing distribution of migrants (figures in '00) by different age-groups for each state/union territory by duration of residence 0-9 years—1971 census

Sex : Male

Age Group	Delhi			Goa, Daman and Diu			Lakshadweep			Pondicherry		
	I	O	I-O	I	O	I-O	I	O	I-O	I	O	I-O
0—2	98	35	+63	22	5	+17	—	—	—	3	15	—12
3—7	321	124	+197	33	16	+17	—	—	—	22	28	—6
8—12	407	138	+269	37	9	+28	—	—	—	19	15	+4
13—17	393	82	+311	28	8	+20	—	—	—	15	9	+6
18—22	794	126	+668	76	38	+38	3	2	+1	19	11	+8
23—27	665	116	+549	73	33	+40	2	—	+2	26	9	+17
28—32	596	124	+472	69	20	+49	—	1	—1	26	11	+15
33—37	311	75	+236	38	10	+28	—	1	—1	15	11	+4
38—42	275	65	+210	30	10	+20	2	—	+2	12	9	+3
43—47	169	36	+133	8	6	+2	—	—	—	8	4	+4
48—52	149	42	+107	15	4	+11	—	—	—	9	9	—
53—57	69	22	+47	5	6	—1	—	—	—	2	1	+1

Age	Delhi			Goa, Daman and Diu			Lakshadweep			Pondicherry		
Group	I	O	I-O	I	O	I-O	I	O	I-O	I	O	I-O
58—62	61	17	+44	11	—	+11	—	—	—	2	6	—4
63—67	23	9	+14	10	—	+10	—	—	—	1	1	—
68—72	25	9	+16	4	2	+2	—	—	—	1	2	—1
73+	30	10	+20	2	2	—	—	—	—	—	—	—
Total	4386	1030	3356	461	169	292	7	4	3	180	141	39

Note: (i) Figures are estimated on 1 per cent sample basis.
(ii) I denotes In-migrants.
(iii) O denotes Out-migrants.
(iv) I-O denotes Net-migrants.

Statement showing distribution of migrants (figures in '00) by different age groups for each state/union territory by duration of residence 0-9 years—1971 census

Sex : Female

Age Group	Andhra Pradesh			Assam			Bihar			Gujarat			Haryana		
	I	O	I-O	I	O	I-O	I	O	I-O	I	O	I-O	I	O	I-O
0—2	77	75	+2	15	21	−6	45	70	−25	84	59	+25	89	68	+21
3—7	220	233	−13	86	67	+19	148	280	−132	208	184	+24	192	175	+17
8—12	216	252	−36	111	74	+37	145	289	−144	151	165	−14	241	193	+48
13—17	204	234	−30	62	64	—2	230	287	−57	124	118	+6	263	241	+22
18—22	515	579	−64	138	106	+32	541	794	−253	375	300	+75	647	533	+114
23—27	301	387	−86	131	77	+54	374	592	−218	299	294	+5	412	362	+50
28—32	176	194	−18	102	64	+38	187	341	−154	179	169	+10	155	151	+4
33—37	79	117	−38	43	23	+20	81	147	−66	61	62	−1	88	75	+13
38—42	78	74	+4	31	23	+8	75	103	−28	61	49	+12	71	45	+26
43—47	44	39	+5	18	17	+1	32	42	−10	37	34	+3	41	41	—
48—52	39	50	−11	17	8	+9	36	53	—17	25	36	—11	32	32	—
53—57	16	24	—8	8	9	—1	15	30	—15	19	15	+4	13	17	—4

APPENDICES—*Contd.*

Age	Andhra Pradesh			Assam			Bihar			Gujarat			Haryana		
Group	I	O	I-O	I	O	I-O	I	O	I-O	I	O	I-O	I	O	I-O
58—62	25	36	—11	12	6	+6	10	40	—30	31	19	+12	21	17	+4
63—67	6	25	—19	11	7	+4	7	13	—6	11	14	—3	8	9	—1
68—72	9	11	—2	5	4	+1	11	16	—5	13	10	+3	4	10	—6
73+	9	8	+1	4	3	+1	6	7	—1	6	12	—6	15	13	+2
Total	2014	2338	—324	794	573	221	1943	3104	1161	1684	1540	144	2292	1982	310

Note: (i) Figures are estimated on 1 per cent sample basis.
(ii) I denotes In-migrants.
(iii) O denotes Out-migrants.
(iv) I-O denotes Net-migrants.

Statement showing distribution of migrants (figures in '00) by different age-groups for each state/union territory by duration of residence 0-9 years—1971 census

Sex : Female

Age	Himachal Pradesh			Jammu and Kashmir			Kerala			Madhya Pradesh			Maharashtra		
Group	I	O	I-O	I	O	I-O	I	O	I-O	I	O	I-O	I	O	I-O
0—2	24	23	+1	6	8	—2	36	71	—35	77	84	—7	229	142	+87
3—7	51	36	+15	20	22	—2	75	142	—67	333	202	+131	621	392	+229
8—12	41	51	—10	15	23	—8	102	128	—26	376	230	+146	575	339	+236
13—17	31	26	+5	13	13	—	67	114	—47	376	293	+83	434	330	+104
18—22	82	102	—20	49	38	+11	122	359	—237	1034	685	+349	1161	668	+493
23—27	88	95	—7	46	25	+21	131	381	—250	628	380	+248	1012	588	+504
28—32	44	30	+14	17	15	+2	65	175	—110	318	204	+114	555	334	+224
33—37	20	24	—4	12	12	—	61	60	+1	176	100	+76	262	149	+113
38—42	11	18	—7	6	6	—	28	56	—28	124	78	+46	175	124	+51
43—47	5	14	—9	5	2	+3	26	34	—8	82	51	+31	102	81	+21
48—52	4	8	—4	3	5	—2	24	39	—15	69	28	+41	109	53	+56
53—57	4	3	+1	—	4	—4	10	16	−6	33	29	+4	63	36	+27

Age Group	Himachal Pradesh			Jammu and Kashmir			Kerala			Madhya Pradesh			Maharashtra		
	I	O	I-O	I	O	I-O	I	O	I-O	I	O	I-O	I	O	I-O
58—62	1	2	—1	1	3	—2	10	20	—10	44	31	+13	74	40	+34
63—67	—	1	—1	—	—	—	6	12	—6	26	17	+9	40	23	+17
68—72	1	3	—2	—	1	—1	4	8	—4	21	16	+5	25	25	—
73+	2	3	—1	—	1	—1	2	5	—3	13	8	+5	27	21	+6
Total	409	439	—30	193	178	15	769	1620	851	3730	2436	1294	5464	3262	2202

Note: (i) Figures are estimated on 1 per cent sample basis.
(ii) I denotes In-migrants.
(iii) O denotes Out-migrants.
(iv) I-O denotes Net-migrants.

Statement showing distribution of migrants (figures in '00) by different age groups for each state/union territory by duration of residence 0-9 years—1971 census

Sex . Female

Age	Manipur			Meghalaya			Mysore			Nagaland			Orissa		
Group	I	O	I-O	I	O	I-O	I	O	I-O	I	O	I-O	I	O	I-O
0—2	—	—	—	5	1	+4	82	115	—33	1	3	—2	54	13	+41
3—7	3	3	—	15	11	+4	273	261	+12	8	2	+6	134	92	+42
8—12	6	4	+2	12	9	+3	280	271	+9	6	8	—2	167	78	+89
13—17	4	3	+1	14	6	+8	254	259	—5	6	2	+4	145	76	+69
18—22	11	7	+4	31	15	+16	612	570	+42	10	7	+3	365	234	+131
23—27	6	4	+2	23	7	+16	389	408	—19	12	—	+12	280	134	+146
28—32	3	4	—1	15	10	+5	252	228	+24	8	1	+7	145	74	+71
33—37	—	2	—2	5	3	+2	113	104	+9	1	—	+1	78	44	+26
38—42	3	1	+2	5	4	+1	84	78	+14	1	2	—1	56	24	+32
43—47	3	—	+3	2	4	—2	49	49	—	1	1	—	38	18	+12
48—52	—	5	—5	—	7	—7	54	52	+2	—	1	—1	22	13	+9
53—57	—	2	—2	3	1	+2	32	24	+8	1	—	+1	17	6	+11

Age	Manipur			Meghalaya			Mysore			Nagaland			Orissa		
Group	I	O	I-O	I	O	I-O	I	O	I-O	I	O	I-O	I	O	I-O
58—62	2	1	+1	2	1	+1	35	33	+2	—	—	—	27	7	+20
63—67	1	—	+1	4	2	+2	25	9	+16	—	1	—1	5	4	+1
68—72	—	—	—	—	1	—1	17	6	+11	—	—	—	11	2	+9
73+	1	—	+1	1	1	—	16	8	+8	—	—	—	10	3	+7
Total	43	36	7	137	83	54	2567	2467	100	55	28	27	1538	822	716

Note: (i) Figures are estimated on 1 per cent sample basis.
(ii) I denotes In-migrants.
(iii) O denotes Out-migrants.
(iv) I-O denotes Net-migrants.

Statement showing distribution of migrants (figures in '00) by different age-groups for each state/union territory by duration of residence 0-9 years—1971 census

Sex : Female

Age	Punjab			Rajasthan			Tamil Nadu			Tripura			Uttar Pradesh		
Group	I	O	I-O	I	O	I-O	I	O	I-O	I	O	I-O	I	O	I-O
0—2	100	93	+7	57	101	—44	96	85	+11	1	1	—	81	207	—126
3—7	196	232	—36	146	273	—127	191	231	—40	3	18	—15	196	549	—353
8—12	201	273	—72	146	295	—149	152	258	—106	11	9	+2	234	543	—309
13—17	168	254	—86	222	267	—45	161	189	—28	8	5	+3	316	509	—193
18—22	460	595	—135	472	808	—336	387	510	—123	11	11	—	860	1611	—751
23—27	320	489	—169	284	450	—166	343	426	—83	10	10	—	495	1145	—650
28—32	163	222	—59	139	223	—84	195	244	—49	12	10	—2	221	646	—425
33—37	61	145	—84	56	96	—40	99	134	—35	2	4	—2	133	289	—156
38—42	48	91	—43	40	87	—47	67	105	—38	2	5	—3	77	194	—117
43—47	30	49	—19	24	55	—31	49	67	—18	—	3	—3	49	100	—51
48—52	31	50	—19	35	40	—5	31	55	—24	3	1	+2	38	101	—63
53—57	12	31	—19	15	19	—4	20	36	—16	1	1	—	28	54	—26

APPENDICES—*Contd.*

Age Group	Punjab I	Punjab O	Punjab I-O	Rajasthan I	Rajasthan O	Rajasthan I-O	Tamil Nadu I	Tamil Nadu O	Tamil Nadu I-O	Tripura I	Tripura O	Tripura I-O	Uttar Pradesh I	Uttar Pradesh O	Uttar Pradesh I-O
58—62	10	33	—23	18	35	—17	24	40	—16	—	2	—2	31	49	—18
63—67	3	12	—9	8	12	—4	13	12	+1	1	1	—	11	25	—14
68—72	9	13	—4	5	13	—8	8	15	—7	1	2	—1	19	26	—7
73+	13	27	—14	6	9	—3	6	16	—10	1	—	+1	13	24	—11
Total	1825	2609	—784	1673	2783	—1110	1842	2423	—581	67	83	—16	2802	6072	—3270

Note: (i) Figures are estimated on 1 per cent sample basis.
(ii) I denotes In-migrants.
(iii) O denotes Out-migrants.
(iv) I-O denotes Net-migrants.

Statement showing distribution of migrants (figures in '00) by different age groups for each state/union territory by duration of residence 0-9 years—1971 census

Sex: Female

Age Group	West Bengal			Andaman & Nicobaa Islands			Arunachal Pradesh			Chandigarh			Dadara & Nagar Haveli		
	O	I	I-O	I	O	I-O	I	O	I-O	I	O	I-O	I	O	I-O
0—2	58	68	—10	1	2	—1	4	—	+4	28	11	+17	3	—	+3
3—7	243	225	+18	5	3	+2	17	3	+14	58	17	+41	4	1	+3
8—12	258	251	+7	7	2	+5	7	1	+6	47	18	+29	5	1	+4
13—17	243	290	—47	2	5	—3	6	3	+3	49	14	+35	6	1	+5
18—22	584	513	+71	9	1	+8	13	1	+12	93	24	+69	16	5	+11
23—27	413	348	+65	13	3	+10	9	3	+6	77	18	+59	7	2	+5
28—32	272	201	+71	8	2	+6	4	2	+2	51	15	+36	1	1	—
33—37	109	111	—2	3	4	—1	4	1	+3	22	7	+15	3	1	+2
38—42	79	86	—7	4	—	+4	3	—	+3	17	10	+7	3	1	+2
43—47	39	48	—9	3	—	+3	2	—	+2	12	1	+11	—	1	—1
48—52	36	38	—2	1	2	—1	2	—	+2	11	2	+9	—	—	—

Age Group	West Bengal			Andaman & Nicober Islands			Arunachal Pradesh			Chandigarh			Dadara & Nagar Haveli		
	O	I	I-O	I	O	I-O	I	O	I-O	I	O	I-O	I	O	I-O
53—57	28	25	+3	—	—	—	—	—	—	7	1	+6	—	1	—1
58—62	21	24	—3	—	—	—	—	—	—	7	1	+6	—	1	—1
63—67	13	13	—	—	—	—	—	—	—	1	—	+1	—	—	—
68—72	15	12	+3	—	1	—1	—	—	—	2	1	+1	1	—	+1
73+	6	13	—7	—	—	—	—	—	—	5	1	+4	—	—	—
Total	2417	2266	151	56	25	31	71	14	57	487	141	+346	49	16	33

Note: (i) Figures are estimated on 1 per cent sample basis.
(ii) I denotes In-migrants.
(iii) O denotes Out-migrants.
(iv) I-O denotes Net-migrants.

Statement showing distribution of migrants (figures in '00) by different age-groups for each state/union territory by duration of residence 0-9 years—1971 census

Sex : Female

Age Group	Delhi			Goa, Daman and Diu			Lakshadweep			Pondicherry		
	I	O	I-O	I	O	I-O	I	O	I-O	I	O	I-O
0—2	112	54	58	19	3	+16	—	—	—	6	12	—6
3—7	312	111	+201	30	15	+19	2	—	+2	16	16	—
8—12	335	130	+205	48	19	+29	—	—	—	28	9	+19
13—17	278	108	+170	35	15	+20	—	—	—	19	14	+5
18—22	718	265	+453	48	39	+9	—	—	—	71	55	+16
23—27	596	199	+397	63	34	+29	1	1	—	60	41	+19
28—32	359	105	+254	31	20	+11	—	—	—	20	15	+5
33—37	176	42	+134	27	15	+12	—	—	—	10	6	+4
38—42	134	37	+97	14	4	+10	—	—	—	11	11	—
43—47	86	22	+64	5	3	+2	—	—	—	2	2	—
48—52	57	12	+45	13	2	+11	—	—	—	3	2	+1
53—57	38	7	+31	9	5	+4	—	—	—	9	3	+6

Age	Delhi			Goa, Daman and Diu			Lakshadweep			Pondicherry		
Group	I	O	I-O	I	O	I-O	I	O	I-O	I	O	I-O
58–62	48	12	+36	4	3	+1	—	—	—	3	5	—2
63—67	15	3	+12	2	1	+1	—	—	—	2	3	—1
68—72	19	4	+15	1	3	+2	—	—	—	2	—	2
73+	26	5	+21	3	2	+1	—	—	—	1	2	—1
Total	3309	1116	2193	352	183	169	3	1	2	263	196	67

Note: (i) Figures are estimated on 1 per cent sample basis.
(ii) I denotes In-migrants.
(iii) O denotes Out-migrants.
(iv) O I denotes Net-migrants.

BIBLIOGRAPHY

Ashish Bose. *Studies in Indian Urbanization, 1970-1971*, Tata McGraw Hill Publishing Co., New Delhi, 1973.

Bouge, Donald J. (1966). *Internal Migration with Special Reference to Rural-Urban Movement*, United Nation World Population Conference, 1965, Belgrade, Vol. I, Summary Report, New York: United Nations.

Bogue, Donald J. and Zachariah, K.C. "Urbanization and Migration in India", R. Turner, ed. *India's Urban Future* (Berkeley: University of California Press, 1962), pp. 27-54.

Burord, R.C. (1962). "An Index of Distance as Related to Internal Migration", *Southern Economic Journal*, 29 (2), pp. 77-81.

Cardwell, John C. (1969), *African Rural-Urban Migration: The Movement to Ghana's Towns*, Columbia University Press, New York.

Davis, Kingsley. "Urbanization in India: Past and Future", *India's Urban Future*, Editor, Turner, Roy (Berkeley and Los Angeles: University of California Press, 1962), Chapter I, pp. 12-26.

Dasgupta, Band, Laishley, R., (1975). "Migration from Villages", *Economic and Political Weekly*, 10 (42): 1952-62.

Eldridge, Hope T. (1964). A Cohort Approach to the Analysis of Migration Differentials, *Demography*, 1: 212-219.

Goodman, Leo A. (1961). Statistical Methods for the Movers-Stayer Model, *Journal of the American Statistical Association*, 56: 841-868.

Greenwood, M.J. (1969). "An Analysis of the Determinants of Geographic Labour Mobility in United States", *Review of Economics and Statistics*, 51: 189-194.

Goldstein Sidney (1976). "Facts of Redistribution: Research Challenges and Opportunities", *Demography*, Vol. 1 3, pp. 423-434.

Government of India. The National Sample Survey: Eighteenth Round: February 1963—January 1964, No. 182, *Tables with Notes on Internal Migration*, 1972.

Hamilton C. Horace (1966). Effects of Census Errors on the Measurement of Net Migration, *Demography*, 3: 393-415.

Hamilton C. Horace, and F.M. Henderson, (1944). Use of the Survival Rate Method in Measuring Net Migration, *Journal of American Statistical Association*, 39: 197-206.

Kuroda, Toshio (1967). *Internal Migration: An Overveiw of Problems and Studies*, World Population Conference, Belgrade, 1965, Vol. IV, New York: United Nations.

Kshirasagar, S. (1973). "Patterns of Internal Migration of Males in India", *Artha Vijnana*, 15 (2); pp. 161-179.

Mahendra K. Premi. "Internal Migration in India", *Population Policy Perspectives in Developing Countries*, Vatsala Narain and C.P. Prakasam, editors, Himalaya Publishing House, Bombay, 1983, pp. 353-372.

National Sample Survey (1960). *No. 56 Tables and Notes on Internal Migration*, Indian Statistical Institute, Calcutta.

P.S. Nair. "Estimation of Directional Migration Flows from Limited Data: Methods and Application", *Working Paper No. 32, Working Paper of the N.I.D.I.*, Voorburg, July 1982.

Price, Daniel O (1955). Examinational Two Sources of Errors in the Estimation of Net Internal Migration, *Journal of the American Statistical Association*, 50: 689-700.

Prabhakara, N.R. "The Pattern of Rural-Urban Internal Migrations: Its Socio-Economic Correlates", *Indian Journal of Labour Economics*, 26 (4), January, 1984.

Pandey, R.B. "Some Aspects of Rural Urban Migration in Bihar", Paper presented in the Indian Census Centenary Seminar, New Delhi, October, 1972.

Pachal, R.K. "Internal Migration in India—Pattern, Implication and Policies", Paper presented at III Annual Conference of I.A.S.P., Osmania University, Hyderabad, 1978.

Ravenotein, E.G. (1885 and 1889). The Laws of Migration,

Journal of the Royal Statistical Society, 48: 167-235; and 52: 241-305.

Rao, G.D. (1973). "Inter-State Migration in India", *Sankhya*, Series-B, No. 35, pp. 367-376.

Rogers, Andrei (1973). Estimating Internal Migration from Incomplete Data Using Multi-regional Life Tables, *Demography*, 10: 277-287.

Singh, S.N.S. and Yadava, K.N.S. (1974). "A Study of Pattern of the Rural-Urban Migration", *Demography India*, 3 (2), 278-286.

Stouffer, S.A. (1940). "Intervening Opportunities: A Theory Relating Mobility and Distance", *American Sociological Review*, 5: 845-867.

Sarkar, B.N. "Development of Indian Economy and Migration", Paper presented in the III Annual Conference of I.A.S.P., Osmania University, Hyderabad, 1978.

Terver, J.D. and McLedo, D.A. (1973). "A Test of Modification of Zipf Hypothesis for Predicting Inter-State Migration", *Demography*, 10: 259-275.

Thomas, D.S. (1928). *Research Memorandum on Migration Differentials, Social Science Research Council Bulletin*, 43, New York.

United Nations (Department of Economic and Social Affairs) (1949). *Problems of Migration Statistics. Population Studies*, No. 5, New York: United Nations.

United Nations (1970). *Methods of Measuring Internal Migration. Manual on the Methods of Estimating Populations, Manual VI.* Population Studies, No. 47, New York: United Nations.

Vaidyanatha, Kunnisery E. (1971). *Components of Urban Growth in India, 1951-61*, International Population Conference, London, 1969, Vol. IV. Liege: International Union for the Scientific Study of Population.

Vaidyanatha, K.R. (1972). "Internal Migration in India: Some Estimates and Relationship", Paper presented at the Session on Internal Migration, Census Centenary Seminar, October 1972, New Delhi.

Zachariah, K.C. (1962). A Note on Census Survival Ratio

Method of Estimating Net Migration, *Journal of the American Statistical Association*, 57: 173-183.

Zachariah, K.C. (1967). *Estimation of Return Migration from Place-of-Birth and Duration-of-Residence Data*, Proceedings of the Sydney Conferences 1967. Liege: International Union for the Scientific Study of Population.

Zachariah, K.C. (1964). *Historical Study of Internal Migration in the Indian Sub-continent 1901-1931*, Asia Publishing House, Bombay.

Zachariah, K.C. (1968). *Migrants in Greater Bombay*, Asia Publishing House, Bombay.

INDEX